"'Religion' is sometimes said to be the root of international conflict; and sometimes a resource for peacemaking. To some, 'religion' underlies human rights abuses; to others, it is the foundation of universal respect and love. But what, actually, is it? Do all these explanations refer to the same thing, or does 'religion' mean different things in different contexts? As Erin K. Wilson demonstrates, such questions have real-world, sometimes even life-and-death, implications. With her trademark clarity, Wilson spells out the policy, legal and international relations implications of how we understand religion, and why it matters".

**Marion Maddox FAHA**,
*Honorary Professor of Politics at Macquarie University, Australia*

"Erin K. Wilson makes a compelling – and highly accessible – case that critical approaches to religion are not the sole preserve of academics, but instead offer great practical insight for practitioners, policymakers, and general audiences alike. Anyone seeking a more nuanced understanding of how religion intersects with contemporary global politics needs to read this book".

**Peter Mandaville**,
*United States Institute of Peace*

"This is a much-needed addition to the growing literature on religion and international politics. Targeting people outside of academia, the book provides guidance on how to study an incredibly complex issue in an admirably clear and straight-forward manner. Drawing on her vast experiences working with policy and civil society over the last decade, Wilson presents her insights and expertise in a way that is accessible and practically applicable. I highly recommend this book for diplomats, NGOs, journalists, legal professionals and anyone else interested in developing a better understanding of religion and global politics".

**Marie Juul Petersen**,
*Danish Human Rights Institute*

"A wonderful new contribution from a scholar permanently committed to connect theory with practice. Erin K. Wilson does not shy away from asking the most critical questions regarding our field of work, but always with the purpose of finding new entry points and exploring new pathways together. Her new book draws on a depth of knowledge on recent scholarship on religion in international relations, from which practitioners like me will benefit for r       to come".

*Program Officer at Mense*

# Religion and World Politics

*Religion and World Politics* provides a short, accessible, and practical introduction to how we can understand the place of religion in world politics in a more comprehensive, contextually relevant way. Is religion central or irrelevant, positive or negative in world politics today? So much political commentary and analysis focuses on these issues. But these are the wrong questions to be asking. Designed for practitioners, policymakers, and newcomers to the topic of religion and global politics, this book emphasises that religion is not something clear, identifiable, and definable, but is fluid and shifting. Consequently, we need analytical frameworks that help us to make sense of this ever-changing phenomenon. The author presents a critical, intersectional framework for analysing religion and applies this to case studies of three core areas of international relations (IR) analysis: (1) conflict, violence, and security; (2) development and humanitarianism; and (3) human rights, law, and public life. These cases highlight how assumptions about what religion is and does affect policymakers, theorists, and activists. The book demonstrates the damage that has been done through policies and programmes based on unquestioned assumptions and the possibilities and insights to be gained by incorporating the critical study of religion into research, policymaking, and practice.

This book will be of great interest to students of global politics, IR, religion, and security studies, as well as diplomats, civil servants, policymakers, journalists, and civil society practitioners. It will also benefit IR scholars interested in developing their research to include religion, as well as scholars of religion from disciplines outside IR interested in a deeper understanding of religion and world politics.

**Erin K. Wilson** is Professor and Chair of Politics and Religion and Vice Dean and Director of Education in the Faculty of Theology and Religious Studies at the University of Groningen, the Netherlands. She is also co-Chair of the Academic Advisory Council for the Transatlantic Partnership Network on Religion and Diplomacy.

# Religion and World Politics
Connecting Theory with Practice

**Erin K. Wilson**

LONDON AND NEW YORK

First published 2022
by Routledge
4 Park Square, Milton Park, Abingdon, Oxon OX14 4RN

and by Routledge
605 Third Avenue, New York, NY 10158

*Routledge is an imprint of the Taylor & Francis Group, an informa business*

© 2022 Erin K. Wilson

The right of Erin K. Wilson to be identified as author of this work has been asserted in accordance with sections 77 and 78 of the Copyright, Designs and Patents Act 1988.

The Open Access version of this book, available at www.taylorfrancis.com, has been made available under a Creative Commons Attribution-Non Commercial-No Derivatives 4.0 license.

 Thanks to the support of libraries working with Knowledge Unlatched www.knowledgeunlatched.org

*Trademark notice*: Product or corporate names may be trademarks or registered trademarks, and are used only for identification and explanation without intent to infringe.

*British Library Cataloguing-in-Publication Data*
A catalogue record for this book is available from the British Library

*Library of Congress Cataloging-in-Publication Data*
Names: Wilson, Erin K., author.
Title: Religion and world politics: connecting theory with practice / Erin K. Wilson.
Description: Abingdon, Oxon; New York, NY: Routledge, 2023. | Includes bibliographical references and index.
Identifiers: LCCN 2022031775 (print) | LCCN 2022031776 (ebook) | Subjects: LCSH: Religion and international relations. | Conflict management—Religious aspects. | Economic development—Religious aspects. | Human rights—Religious aspects. Classification: LCC BL65.I55 W55 2023 (print) | LCC BL65.I55 (ebook) | DDC 201/.72—dc23/eng/20220802
LC record available at https://lccn.loc.gov/2022031775
LC ebook record available at https://lccn.loc.gov/2022031776

ISBN: 978-0-367-47866-7 (hbk)
ISBN: 978-0-367-68405-1 (pbk)
ISBN: 978-1-003-03705-7 (ebk)

DOI: 10.4324/9781003037057

Typeset in Times New Roman MT Std
by codeMantra

# Contents

| | | |
|---|---|---|
| *Preface* | | viii |
| 1 | Unlearning Religion as (We Think) We Know It | 1 |
| 2 | Relearning Religion: Connecting Theory with Practice | 18 |
| 3 | The Things We Fear: Religion in Conflict, Violence, and Security | 32 |
| 4 | From Secular Development to Global Partnership: Religion in International Aid and Humanitarianism | 62 |
| 5 | Myths of Equality and Neutrality: Religion in Human Rights, Law, and Public Life | 92 |
| | Conclusion | 121 |
| | *Bibliography* | 125 |
| | *Index* | 141 |

# Preface

I first began studying religion and International Relations (IR) over two decades ago. Like many scholars who emerged in the post-9/11 era, I focused on religion out of a recognition that IR was missing something when it came to this important topic. Exactly what we were missing, though, and how to study it more holistically, was something I, at least, had little to no idea about. That is, of course, why we do the work. If we had the answers, there would be no need for the questions. To enhance our understanding of this phenomenon we call "religion", we sought insights from adjacent disciplines such as anthropology, philosophy, sociology, law, and gender studies, learning from these scholars and incorporating their insights into our theories of IR.

This book is an attempt to present a systematic and hopefully clear and comprehensible approach to studying religion and world politics in a critical, intersectional, contextually sensitive way. It builds on the insights that have been generated in the past two decades by a cohort of scholars all trying to figure out how IR can more effectively study religion. The book aims to make clear for students, policymakers, practitioners, and anyone else who might be interested why we need these alternative approaches, what it is that distinguishes this new generation of scholarship from that which came before and how these approaches address the errors and shortcomings of previous thinking that has contributed to serious mistakes in security policy, military strategy, aid and development programming, and human rights advocacy.

In my view, the recognition that religion is not an object "out there" that is clearly identifiable, definable, and measurable, but rather a fluid, dynamic, and ever-changing category made up of rituals, practices, discourses, narratives, institutions, organisations, actors, beliefs, and norms that are all context-dependent and variable is one of the most revolutionary insights we have gained from this scholarship. It has the potential to transform our analysis and our policymaking, enabling

*Preface* ix

it to be more sensitive and responsive to real-world dynamics, more reflective, and more collaborative, as I attempt to demonstrate in the pages that follow.

Fundamentally, recognising that "religion" is a category that holds different meanings for different people in different contexts across time and space is a recognition that we do not and cannot know what "religion" is. We do not and cannot know everything that there is to know about "religion", "secularism", and how these categories and insights operate everywhere and for all time. Recognising this requires that we approach each new situation where "religion" is present with curiosity and a desire to learn from those who inhabit the spaces we are exploring.

This book presents an overview of what the study of religion in world politics can contribute if we take this critical understanding of "religion" as our point of departure. It is a stocktake of how far we have come, a grateful acknowledgement of the work of a talented generation of critical religion and IR scholars, and a recognition that there is yet more to be done. We are at a significant juncture for the field and for global politics more generally, where religion has become a crucial component of identity and power politics being played out on the world stage. We need careful, nuanced, contextually embedded analysis of religious actors, dynamics, discourses, and practices and their interactions with security, human rights, law, gender, development, humanitarianism, and climate change. Hopefully, this book helps to guide these future investigations and contributions.

No one ever writes a book on their own, no matter what it says on the front cover. I signed the contract to write this book one month before starting as Vice Dean and Director of Education in my Faculty, and four months before the start of the worst pandemic in a century. Consequently, writing this book was harder and required more concerted focus and effort than I had anticipated. But then everything about 2020 and 2021 was harder than any of us anticipated.

As such, I want to thank Hannah Rich and Emily Ross at Routledge for their support, patience, and understanding every time I emailed to request yet another extension of the submission deadline, and to Hannah for providing feedback on portions of the text.

Second, my thanks to Jenny Edkins for inviting me to contribute the chapter on religion for the *Routledge Handbook of Critical International Relations*, which inspired me to write this volume.

This project has become increasingly important for me as I have worked on it. I did not want to write just another book on religion and IR. I wanted to offer something particularly for those new to the

x *Preface*

topic – students, diplomats, civil servants, civil society practitioners, journalists – a clear and for the most part practical guide to thinking differently about religion and international politics, and how to operationalise that in research, policymaking, reporting, legislation, project design and implementation. What I present in this book is imperfect and by no means the only or even best way of critically researching and analysing religion in IR, but it's a start. In developing these ideas I have drawn inspiration from how colleagues and peers studying religion in global politics conduct their research, and I wish to acknowledge them for their innovation, creativity, and wisdom in pioneering this work: Kim Knibbe, Elizabeth Shakman Hurd, Lori Beaman, Marie Juul Petersen, Susan Hayward, Evan Berry, Helge Årsheim, Cecelia Lynch, Luca Mavelli, Matthew Nelson, Stacey Gutkowski, Jeremy, Menchik, Rouzbeh Parsi, Méadhbh McIvor, Julia Martínez-Ariño, Brenda Bartelink, Brenda Mathijssen, Vivienne Matthies-Boon, Merete Bilde, and Judd Birdsall. Peter Mandaville deserves special mention for reading the whole manuscript, multiple times, and providing precise, constructive feedback. Other scholars and friends important to the project include Roland Bleiker, Emma Hutchison, Toby Volkman, Vanessa Sequeira, Nicholas Monsbourgh, Eva Slot, Mladen Popović, Nienke Bastiaans, Monica Duffy-Toft, Elena Mucciarelli, Barbara Brink, Chris and Gnat Matthews, Courtney Bonneau, Jess Mills, Megan Embry, Rhiannon Bruce, Marion Maddox, Jülide Kaynihan, Ton Groeneweg, and Eva Krah.

Special thanks to my research assistants Linde Draaisma and Ilse van Tuinen.

I am especially grateful to the Knowledge Unlatched Foundation, whose generous support enabled the Open Access publication of the book, and the Netherlands Scientific Research Council (NWO) for the Aspasia Grant that facilitated research for components of the manuscript.

Portions of the material in Chapters 4 and 5 were previously published in two journal articles: Grüll, C.M. and E.K. Wilson. 2018. "Universal or Particular or Both? The Right to Freedom of Religion or Belief in Cross-Cultural Contexts" *Review of Faith and International Affairs* 16(4): 88–101, Taylor & Francis, and Wilson, E.K. 2022. "Blurring Boundaries or Deepening Discourses: From Global to Local and Back Again" *The Review of Faith and International Affairs* 20(2): 69–80, Taylor & Francis. Adapted here with permission.

Photos provided by Courtney Bonneau, Brenda Bartelink, and Mensen met een Missie and original drawings provided by Jessica Mills Designs are used with permission.

*Preface*  xi

As always, my thanks to my family, Cam, Karen and Jeremy Wilson, Lynne Doneley, Sheena Polkinghorne, Ann Cheetham, the Hall family, especially Helen and Joanna, for their love and support (especially Mum, who read the draft manuscript with a critical eye), and my husband Phil Monsbourgh, for always encouraging and believing in me, especially when I don't believe in myself.

# 1 Unlearning Religion as (We Think) We Know It

- *Is the Ukraine-Russia conflict religious?*
- *Are the Taliban a religious organisation?*
- *Are religion and human rights incompatible?*
- *Is religious extremism different from other extremisms?*
- *Is religion violent or peaceful?*
- *Is religion relevant to international politics, or is it merely a tool used by political leaders for their own agendas?*

Some of these questions no doubt sound familiar. You may have heard people asking questions like this or even asked them yourself. Some of them are questions that scholars of religion and world politics have been grappling with for decades, in some cases centuries.

There are, however, two key problems with these questions. The first is perhaps obvious – they're closed questions, inviting only a "yes or no", "either or" response. As any good researcher or educator will tell you, we should start with open questions that invite curiosity and allow for multiple perspectives and answers.

The second problem with these questions, though, is that they all imply a pre-existing understanding of what "religion" itself is. They suggest a fixed, established standard or criteria for determining whether something is "religious" or not. They imply that we can figure out and make a distinction between what is "religion" and what is "politics". These questions also assume that "religion" means the same thing in different contexts. They depart from a particular idea about what "religion" is, usually grounded in Euro-American experiences of Christianity, and seek to determine whether different phenomena in international politics are "religious" or not, or whether religion is a help or hindrance in pursuing peace, sustainable development, and human rights, according to this pre-existing idea.

DOI: 10.4324/9781003037057-1

## 2  *Unlearning Religion as (We Think) We Know It*

Starting with a fixed idea of religion and using it to examine diverse contexts, events, and issues in international politics is a bit like trying to make a square peg fit into a round hole. As religious studies scholars have long understood, "religion" is not fixed and unchanging but dynamic and fluid, meaning different things and manifesting in different ways across different times and places. This means that to develop a comprehensive nuanced appreciation for religion's role in international politics, we must move away from preconceived notions about what religion is. Instead, we must depart from a focus on context, exploring what "religion" means within specific settings, in relation to particular issues, for the diverse actors involved, engaging with religion as it is lived and experienced by real people in their everyday realities.

This book presents a framework for analysing religion and world politics that enables us to do just that. It is intended as an introduction to thinking about religion and world affairs differently, as well as a practical guide for how we can do that, for students of international relations (IR), policymakers, civil society practitioners, and anyone interested in developing a more comprehensive way of understanding the place of religion in the contemporary political, security, and humanitarian landscapes. Drawing on critical and intersectional theoretical insights, combined with "lived religion" approaches from religious studies (Berger, Buitelaar and Knibbe 2021), the book demonstrates that what we think we know about religion rests on unstable conceptual ground. Rather than resolving this instability, the book suggests that we accept and work with it, developing analytical frameworks that help us make sense of what "religion" means in different contexts, at different times, on different issues, for different actors.

For the remainder of this introductory chapter, I sketch the contours of prevailing approaches to the question of religion's role and influence in world politics. I include a brief overview of different secularisms that have shaped the study of religion in IR. These different secularisms give form to prevailing analytical approaches that assume that "religion" is *something*, a clearly identifiable and definable object and agent for analysis. Despite their differences, these secularist approaches all tend to result in analyses that either over- or under-emphasise religion's significance in world politics and characterise it as either "good" or "bad". I demonstrate the consequences of these assumptions through a discussion of IR analysis of the ongoing conflict in Ukraine.

## Close Encounters of the Coffee Kind

I first began thinking about developing this framework in 2014. I had been invited to present a paper on "The Future of Religion" at a workshop in Oxford. The workshop was one in a series of gatherings organised to provide input for the Global Trends report, a publicly sourced and available report produced every four years by the US National Intelligence Council (NIC). The report is designed to provide a strategic assessment of global trends for the next 20 years to assist incoming presidential administrations with long-term policy planning. I found the idea of providing a strategic assessment on the future of religion both intriguing and puzzling, to say the least. Which religion were the NIC interested in? What region of the world did they want to know about? Were they interested in religious institutions, community and non-government organisations, or individual believers? Did they want to know about internal religious dynamics, or how religion interacted with specific socio-political issues (and if so which issues)? There is only so much that can be covered in a 10-minute presentation. When I asked about these specifics, the scope became ever so slightly less broad – now I was told to speak about what I thought would happen with religion in international politics in the future.

In the end, I decided to give a presentation on the future of relationships between government and religious actors. I argued that how senior US policy officials decided to define what "religion" was – how state agencies chose to engage with religious actors (indeed, who they even identified as "religious actors"), who they decided to include and exclude from projects and dialogues about "religious issues", where they decided to incorporate attention for religious dynamics and where they chose to ignore it – would have as much influence on the future of religion in global politics as dynamics on the ground within and amongst religious communities, institutions, and organisations themselves.

My presentation was met with confusion from the policymakers in the room. They were perplexed and, I suspect, irritated by my emphasis on the numerous complex factors and dynamics that I argued should be taken into consideration when analysing religion. The analysts in the room appreciated that it was complex but needed a "framework" for how to address religion in policymaking. Over coffee afterwards, one of them commented to me, "I think the question of how to define religion is interesting for academics, but it isn't really relevant for policymakers".

# 4 *Unlearning Religion as (We Think) We Know It*

Central to this "cross-cultural encounter" between the worlds of academia and policymaking – frustrating on both sides – was a fundamental difference in our understanding of what religion is. In much of the policy world, the prevailing understanding of religion resembles that which underpinned the questions at the start of this chapter, that it is singular, fixed, and unchanging. We know religion when we see it. Sure, there are *different* religions, but they all share certain basic characteristics and operate in much the same way when it comes to analysing broader trends in global politics. For a long time, this view was also the dominant understanding of religion within academia, in any discipline beyond religious studies, including IR. Religion was considered irrelevant at best, dangerous at worst, and should be kept out of the realm of politics altogether. Thus, it was marginalised or ignored in studies of global politics (Hurd 2008; Mavelli 2012; Wilson 2012).

This essentialist approach to religion and global politics has been robustly challenged in recent years. Rather than being a fixed, taken-for-granted object for study, alternative perspectives have emerged that describe religion as a category of understanding and analysis, one that is filled with different meanings and assumptions depending on the context and the actors involved. Scholars positing this perspective draw on insights from religious studies, anthropology, sociology, philosophy, gender studies, and law, amongst others, to highlight that "religion" – as both a category for analysis and a socio-political, cultural phenomenon – is never static. It is constantly shaping and being shaped by the actors and institutions with which it interacts and intervenes. Contrary to the assertion by my coffee companion in Oxford, these scholars argue that how to define religion is central to the work of policymakers because, whether they realise it or not, they are constantly defining and re-defining religion through the policies and laws they draft and implement, with real and sometimes dire consequences for people's everyday lives. As I responded to my colleague at the time, "I think how to define religion is relevant for policymakers, but it's my job as an academic to demonstrate how, when and why it matters", a task I undertake in the following pages.

## International Relations' Religion Epiphany

It has become common in recent years for scholars, diplomats, and civil society practitioners to enthusiastically declare that "religion is back". Religion has surprised everyone by refusing to quietly fade into the mists of time, instead reasserting itself as a powerful force in the 21st century.

*Unlearning Religion as (We Think) We Know It*   5

Such pronouncements reveal some peculiar underlying assumptions. For one thing, they imply that "religion" had actually retreated from global politics, when arguably it has always been present and relevant, just dismissed or ignored by scholars and analysts. For another, it suggests that "religion" *decided* to make a comeback, implying that "religion" somehow has agency to choose whether it wants to be active in world politics or not.

But what exactly are we talking about when we say that "religion is back"? Are we talking about religious believers, institutions, doctrine, ephemeral transcendent phenomena? What is it that makes something a "religion" and not, say, a political ideology, worldview, or lifestyle? And what was it about the late 20th and early 21st century that prompted "religion", whatever it is, to decide to come back?

At the heart of these declarations from scholars and policymakers about religion's return sits an idea of "religion" as a clearly identifiable object or agent that we can label, identify, and analyse. Questioning this foundational assumption is at the core of critical approaches to the study of religion and world politics. In the same way that critical scholars of race, gender, and class do not take these categories for granted, but explore the meanings they are endowed with by different actors in different settings, so too do critical religion scholars examine the power relations that are bound up in the meanings and usages of the category of religion. Rather than examining what "religion" does in world politics, they instead ask what "religion" means, who gets to decide, why they decide on one meaning over another and what the consequences are of using certain understandings of religion over others for policy, law, practice, and the lives of individuals and communities on the ground.

## Unlearning Religion

The goal of this book is to synthesise these recent critiques of secularist approaches to religion in IR into a framework for the critical, intersectional study of religion and world politics. The central argument of the book is three-fold: First, and perhaps counterintuitively, that scholars, policymakers, and practitioners interested in understanding religion in world affairs need to *not* begin their analysis by focusing on "religion". Rather, analysis needs to depart from the specific issue or context and explore what "religion" means in that situation. Second, that "religion" should not be analysed in isolation but must be considered in connection with other socio-political factors such as class, race, gender, environment, and so on. Third, rather than just

## 6    *Unlearning Religion as (We Think) We Know It*

referring to "religion", we need to be more precise about what we mean when we use this term. We need to highlight the actors, narratives, and identities connected with the category of "religion", as well as which religious tradition we are referring to, within the parameters of the context or issue being analysed.

Such an approach requires that we "unlearn" everything we think we know about what religion is and how it operates in world politics. "Religion" is not a fixed, unchanging, clearly identifiable object or agent for analysis. It is a dynamic, fluid category of meaning that shifts and changes depending on the situation, the actors involved, the issues at stake and, most importantly, the power relations at play.

### Victor Hugo: Celebrated Author, National Hero, or Sacred Prophet?[1]

This diversity of what "religion" is amongst different actors in different contexts will become evident throughout the cases discussed in this book. Nonetheless, it is perhaps helpful to immediately consider a brief concrete example – the identity and legacy of 19th-century French author Victor Hugo. In 21st-century Anglo-American contexts, Hugo is perhaps best known as the author of novels such as *Les Miserables* and *Notre Dame de Paris*, books that have inspired smash-hit musicals and films. In France, he is revered as one of the most important French Romantic writers, remembered both for his political writings that advocated liberty and republicanism and for his collections of poetry, particularly *Les Contemplations*, written after the death of his daughter Léopoldine (Barrère 2022). In Southern Vietnam, his writings were inspirational for the anti-colonial struggle against French imperial rule (Walthausen 2019). In addition to all these manifestations, however – visionary author, defender of republicanism, revolutionary thinker – Hugo is also a saint within Caodaism, a "new religious movement" that emerged in Vietnam (then French Indochina) in 1926 (Hoskins 2007; see Figure 1.1). Since then, Caodaism has dispersed globally, primarily through the Vietnamese diaspora (Hoskins 2015). Within Cao Dai, it is not Hugo's poetry or his expansive novels that are most revered, but the transcripts of séances he held during his period of exile from France, in which, amongst other things, he predicted the emergence of a new unifying religion (Walthausen 2019).

Hugo's legacy within Cao Dai is complex and attributable to numerous factors. Cao Dai has at times been described by scholars as mainly a "peasant political movement" (Hoskins 2007) rather than a religion, owing to its focus on the struggle against French colonial

*Figure 1.1* Painting from Tay Ninh Temple: *The Three Saints of Cao Dai.*
(L-R) Sun Yat-sen, Victor Hugo and Nguyễn Bỉnh Khiêm, signing
a covenant between God and humanity.

Source: Nic Saigon, https://commons.wikimedia.org/wiki/File:CaoDai_3Saints.jpg,
CC BY-SA 3.0.

rule. Hugo's satirical political writings against Napoleon III are considered influential here. Yet this interpretation as a political movement sidelines Cao Dai's spiritual elements. Cao Dai adherents consider it to be an expression of "cosmopolitan spirituality", blending elements of Chinese literature, Theravada Buddhism, Taoist occultism, and Euro-American spiritualists (Hoskins 2007) – for example, other figures such as Joan of Arc, Rene Descartes, Lenin, and Shakespeare are

## 8 *Unlearning Religion as (We Think) We Know It*

also considered Cao Dai saints (Hoskins 2007). Alongside the humanist values at the core of his novels, it is in this "cosmopolitan spirituality" that the mysticism of Hugo's séances has, according to scholars and observers, had the most significant influence, shaping the values represented by Caodaism.

The example of Victor Hugo and Cao Dai helps us to see concretely how different people, objects, practices, and so on, can be seen as "religious" or not, depending on the context. In France, Hugo is a celebrated writer and advocate of French Republicanism, noted for its "secular" character. In Cao Dai, he is a saint. Thus, whether Hugo is a "religious" figure or not depends very much on who we ask, where we look and how we define "religion". It also shows that analytical frameworks that separate the "political" from the "religious" do not allow us to fully appreciate the intricacies of Cao Dai, which is arguably a politico-religious movement. This ambiguous status between political and/or religious movement has further resulted in challenges for adherents of the movement. In Vietnam, while Cao Dai is recognised as a religion by the Vietnamese government, leaders and individual adherents still experience harassment and persecution from Vietnamese authorities. This is in part because of the movement's affiliation with political revolutionary movements of the past and in part because of its status as a minority religion, yet it is impossible to determine whether such instances of harassment take place because of religion, ethnicity, or politics (US State Department 2022). In this example, we see that religion is not separate and distinct from other spheres of human activity, but inextricably entangled with the colonial history, Cold War political legacy, and domestic political, ethnic, and religious tensions within Vietnam today. These intricacies have not always been given space or attention in dominant approaches to religion in IR.

### Religion and International Relations: The Story So Far…

The study of religion in IR has grown exponentially in the post-Cold War period. For much of the history of IR, religion was simply not considered. As Kubalkova (2013) argues, IR is a secular discipline. Dominant theoretical paradigms assumed that religion had been removed from the public sphere and from the political affairs of states. Thus, religion was a domestic issue for states and a private matter for their citizens. Religion did not, could not, or should not feature in IR analysis. The dominant realist paradigm also privileged a focus on material factors affecting national interest, security, and power. Less tangible factors such as gender, race, class, culture, language, and religion for the most part were not given space or attention.

*Unlearning Religion as (We Think) We Know It* 9

The consequence of this long-term neglect was that IR was ill-equipped for analysing religion when it appeared to "return" to international politics (although in reality, it never went away). While immense advances have been made regarding scholarship on the topic, these nuanced insights have remained largely confined to scholarly debates. In the attitudes of political leaders, diplomats, and media, with a few rare exceptions, approaches to and understandings of religion in international politics continue to be shaped by, at best, superficial assumptions and understandings of what religion is and does. These assumptions stem from deeply embedded biases, connected to worldviews shaped by secularism.

While there are numerous definitions and interpretations of secularism, I focus here on secularisms that have been described by multiple scholars as forms of political ideology (Asad 2003; Hurd 2008; Kuru 2009; Philpott 2009; Casanova 2011; Mavelli 2012; Wilson 2012; Mahmood 2016) positing specific normative attitudes and assumptions about what "religion" is and what its role in politics and public life should be. There is debate as to whether secularism is best understood as an ideology, a paradigm, a worldview, or all of these, depending on the historical, political, and cultural context under consideration. Nonetheless, scholars agree that there are different kinds of secularisms, and that context matters when exploring how these different kinds of secularisms shape policy approaches to religion and politics.

Political secularisms are concerned with the role that religion should have in public life and how to manage this role. They primarily focus on two core issues: the significance of religion for public life (whether it is central or marginal) and the type of influence religion exercises (whether it is positive or negative). Different political secularisms are founded on different perspectives on these core issues, yet they share the core foundational assumption that "religion" is something that we can clearly label and identify. Several scholars have developed terminology and typologies for differentiating these diverse political secularisms (Hurd 2008; Kuru 2009; Philpott 2009). For the sake of clarity, I use Kuru's (2009) terminology of passive and assertive secularisms.

Passive secularisms either do not have especially strong views about religion's significance for public life or hold the view that religion can be a positive influence in public life, within certain parameters, and contribute to the common good. States that are governed predominantly by passive secularism may allow or even foster public expressions of religion and involvement of religious organisations in public life. These kinds of involvement could include anything from the provision of welfare and public services to political campaigning. The US is often highlighted as an example of passive secularism (Kuru 2009).

## 10  *Unlearning Religion as (We Think) We Know It*

Often, however, passively secular states do not view all religions in the same positive light. Another consequence of secular ideologies is that within the category of "religion", a hierarchy between different "religions" exists. Thus, the contributions of some religious groups to politics and public life are viewed more favourably than those of other religious groups. In passively secular contexts in Europe and North America, Christianity is often deemed a positive presence in public life, part of the liberal democratic values and cultural heritage of these regions (Beaman 2013). Christian presence in public life is permitted and at times even encouraged, while the public presence of other religions and especially of Islam is discouraged and limited. By contrast, Hinduism is the religion in India that holds the most privileged position when it comes to hierarchies of public religions (Nelson 2020a). In Indonesia, it is Islam (Menchik 2015; Grüll and Wilson 2018). Thus, while passive secularisms may not assiduously exclude all religion from the public sphere, they are also not neutral regarding how they perceive and value different religious traditions and communities. This highlights the importance of not simply referring to "religion" in our analysis. We must be specific about the tradition and community within the category of "religion" that we are referring to.

In contrast to passive secularisms, assertive secularisms actively police the boundaries of the public sphere to exclude religion. Whether they consider religion's influence central or marginal, assertive secularisms are imbued with the perspective that religion is potentially dangerous, disruptive, irrational, and a source of violence, division, and chaos when permitted in the public sphere. Consequently, all elements of religion, including expressions of religious belief such as the wearing of religious symbols, should be excluded from politics and public life. An example of this kind of secularism is the legislation introduced since the early 2000s by several European states, including the Netherlands,[2] France,[3] and Belgium,[4] to ban the wearing of religious symbols in public, or the bans against face coverings, which more explicitly target Muslim women.

These kinds of secularisms are not only influential at the level of domestic state politics. Scholars who have studied secularism in world politics note that these political secularisms have also shaped the way religion is studied in IR. The core issues driving such analyses are religion's significance (whether it is central or marginal) and the type of influence it wields (positive or negative). What this produces in the end is an analytical framework that is limited to little more than statements about religion's centrality or marginality alongside assertions about its "good" or (far more frequently) "bad" disposition (see Figure 1.2).

*Unlearning Religion as (We Think) We Know It*  11

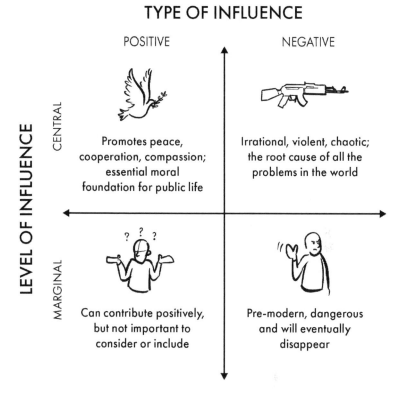

*Figure 1.2* Secularist approaches to Religion and World Politics.
Image Credit: Jessica Mills Designs.

These analytical tendencies are acutely obvious in recent examinations of the Russia-Ukraine conflict. For the most part, analyses published in prominent newspapers and by high-profile IR scholars exhibits an "all or nothing" approach to religion. Commentaries by prominent realist scholars such as John Mearsheimer (2014) and Henry Kissinger (2014), for example, either do not mention religion at all or, if they do, only mention it in passing, almost as a quaint feature of the cultural and political identities in this region of the world. A forum on the Harvard Kennedy School website dedicated to analysis of the conflict contains no articles that provide a sustained treatment of the place of religion in the conflict. These analyses all focus on the geopolitics of the region: Russian concerns about NATO expansion and military build-up; access to and control over oil and gas supplies;

## 12  *Unlearning Religion as (We Think) We Know It*

speculation that Russia under Putin is seeking to expand its territory back to what it was during the Cold War, driven by pure power politics calculations, coupled with an understanding of Ukraine as essentially part of Russia; and cyber-security and economic consequences of the conflict. Religion, if it receives a mention at all, is either mentioned as part of Russia's understanding of history – the importance of Ukraine as the historical source of "Russian religion" (Kissinger 2014) – or highlighted as part of Putin's heavy emphasis on civilisational identity and Russia as the defender of Christianity (Thames 2022).

This mention of civilisations provides an insight as to why many scholars and analysts may be reluctant to address the topic of religion in relation to Ukraine. Over the past three decades, analyses of security issues and conflicts where religion is invoked have often been tainted by association with Samuel Huntington's highly influential yet dubious theory about the "Clash of Civilisations" (CoC). This theory epitomises the kind of approach that makes "religion" central to conflict, violence, and insecurity in world politics, yet dangerously obscures important nuances, contributing to policy missteps. Huntington (1993) posited that in the post-Cold War era, conflicts would no longer be primarily driven by nation-states or by economic or territorial interest. Rather, civilisations would become the primary defining units for parties to conflicts. While somewhat vague and loosely defined, culture and particularly religion were central to Huntington's conceptualisation of "civilisations". His treatment of "religion" and how it maps on to the various civilisations he identifies is, as Robert Kelly (2022) has put it, "lazy and reductionist". His description of Islam as a singular civilisational entity erases the substantial differences between how Muslims engage with and manifest their faith in the Middle East and South Asia, for example. It completely overlooks the multiple types of Islam (Sunni, Shia, Sufi, Ahmadiyya, to name a few) that exist within these diverse regions. Further, CoC theory pays no attention to the diverse ways these multifarious Islams are entangled with politics, national identity, history, and culture in these heterogeneous regions of the world. Scholars have made similar criticisms of Huntington's treatment of the so-called "Orthodox" civilisation. As Olivier Roy (2022) pointed out, the war in Ukraine provides definitive proof that the CoC theory does not work, because Huntington's theory predicted that Orthodox Christian countries would not go to war against one another. This sweeping generalisation ignores the substantial variations within Orthodox Christianity. It also treats religion as a category separate from national identity, when in many countries where Orthodox

*Unlearning Religion as (We Think) We Know It* 13

Christianity is dominant, the specific tradition of Orthodoxy is often distinguished in national terms (Leustean 2022).

Despite these obvious flaws and widespread criticism, CoC theory remains influential within the public imagination. For many years, CoC provided the broader interpretive framework for security policy in the post-9/11 years, with damaging consequences for Muslim populations within Europe and North America and for relations with countries with large Muslim populations (Suleman 2018; Bullock 2022). Putin's framing and justification of the Russian invasion of Ukraine has invoked notions of civilisation and shared spiritual heritage between Russia and Ukraine (Kozelsky 2014, 219; O'Beara 2022), prompting something of a revival of CoC theory in analysis and commentary on the conflict. Some analysts argue that a CoC is precisely what Putin wants (Meaney 2022), while others suggest that while Huntington's theory might have been wrong on some specific dimensions of world politics, it nonetheless provides a useful roadmap for understanding the direction in which world politics is headed (Douthat 2022).

What is observable in these prominent analyses of the conflict in Ukraine is that "religion" is treated as a distinct entity, separate from political, economic, or strategic concerns. It is linked to culture and identity, yet largely undefined and unnuanced. This leads to a preponderance of analyses where attention for religious dynamics is completely absent, or else centralised in such a generalised and reductionist way as to be unhelpful to the point of damaging and dangerous. Further, they all start from a kind of "top-down" approach to analysing religion in the conflict, imposing an abstract external conceptualisation of religion and focusing on geopolitical factors first, rather than paying attention to the dynamics taking place on the ground in situ.

Yet there are alternative treatments of the conflict in Ukraine that pay attention to religious dynamics without essentialising or overemphasising them. These analyses do not suggest that religion is the primary explanatory factor for the conflict in Ukraine, but neither do they marginalise or ignore its significance for the actors involved. For example, while Kozelsky (2014, 220) states that religion's role in the conflict should not be underestimated, she is also careful to emphasise that this doesn't mean that Orthodoxy motivates violence. Rather, she specifies, "religious belief has framed the way many Russians and Ukrainians regard each other". Already this analysis offers a point of distinction with the "all or nothing" approaches – Kozelsky does not just use the blanket term "religion", but is careful to differentiate that she is referring to "religious beliefs", and later also specifically engaging with the role of

14  *Unlearning Religion as (We Think) We Know It*

religious institutions. She connects her analysis to the historical and political context of both Russia and Ukraine, and she discusses the intricacies and diversity of the Orthodox Church in both countries, not simply referring to the "Orthodox World". Similarly, Kalenychenko and Brylov (2022) focuse specifically on the reactions of Ukrainian religious actors to the conflict, not just a generalised notion of "religion". Their analysis is carefully situated within Ukrainian politics, culture, demography, and history. In doing so, they identify additional points of tension that may exacerbate the conflict, as well as highlighting possible avenues for conflict resolution and peacebuilding. For example, Kalenychenko and Brylov (2022) note "an overall culture of competition", the use of "hate speech in everyday communication", and religious and political leaders' "mutual instrumentalisation" of each other as factors that could exacerbate intra- and inter-religious tensions and impede the important work that religious actors are doing in responding to the broader social and community needs amidst the conflict. Other analyses (e.g. Mandaville 2022) highlight (and take seriously) the intersection of religious narratives and identities with geopolitical strategic goals. European Union (EU) leaders have explored "religious diplomacy", through high-profile religious leaders including Pope Francis and the Archbishop of Canterbury, as well as via the international and EU affairs branches of both the Catholic and Orthodox Churches (O'Beara 2022).

In none of these analyses is "religion" presented as the primary reason for the conflict. Yet, by embedding their investigations within the specific context and specifying more clearly what aspect of "religion" they are examining, these studies provide a more nuanced and holistic picture of the relationship between religious, political, cultural, historical, and economic dynamics in the crisis in Ukraine than standard dominant approaches (see Table 1.1).

*Table 1.1*  A comparison of dominant and critical approaches to religion and IR

| Standard "Secular" Approaches | Critical Approaches |
| --- | --- |
| Religion irrelevant or central cause of conflict | Religion present, but balanced |
| External, abstract, generalised, reductionist conceptualisation of religion, with little reference to context | Contextually embedded, nuanced, understanding of religious dynamics |
| "Religion" separated from other factors | "Religion" entangled with other factors |
| Undifferentiated discussion of "religion" | Specification of focus on religious actors, identities, narratives |

*Unlearning Religion as (We Think) We Know It* 15

## What's Next?

In the following chapters, I develop these preliminary insights from critical approaches to religion in the Ukraine conflict into a framework – as asked for by my Oxford interlocutors – for how we might analyse religion in global politics and apply it to three core areas of IR: security and conflict, development and humanitarianism, and human rights and public life. Chapter 2 presents the framework, which rests on three main principles: first, that context is crucial; second, that the category of religion should not be analysed in isolation but rather in its intersections with other categories such as politics, gender, environment, economics, class, race, and so on; third, that rather than speak of "religion", our language needs to be more precise. Not only do we need to be clear about which religious tradition we are referring to, we also need to be specific regarding the phenomena we are highlighting. We need to break the category of "religion" down further. I propose three sub-categories – religious actors, religious identities, and religious narratives – and describe what each of these sub-categories includes. Central to this analytical framework is the consideration of the power relationships that exist between and amongst religious actors and other socio-political agents, which religious identities are privileged and marginalised, and the influence ascribed to certain narratives over others. Understanding these power relationships further helps us to appreciate that how religion is understood within specific contexts impacts the lived experiences of individuals and communities.

Chapter 3 engages with what some scholars consider to be the "core business" of IR: analysing conflict, security, and extremism. The chapter argues that the production of religion as an object of fear continues to be a central structuring logic in approaches to analysing conflicts where religion is involved. Fear of religion leads to misunderstanding of its significance in conflict settings. As we have already touched upon in the Ukraine case, either religion's role is over-emphasised and the conflict is characterised as "religious" or it is under-emphasised and understanding religion in context is largely absent from any strategic analysis or response. Both approaches contribute to limiting policy options and may result in interventions that exacerbate rather than diffuse tensions around conflict. The chapter considers the coup and ongoing civil and political unrest in Myanmar, the aftermath of recent conflicts in Iraq, and the transnational rise of right-wing extremism to make explicit how reductionist approaches to religion in IR contribute to making us more insecure, rather than less, and how approaching religion and conflict from a critical intersectional perspective provides

16 *Unlearning Religion as (We Think) We Know It*

possibilities for more holistic analysis of conflicts and violence and subsequently a broader array of policy options for how to respond to and resolve such crisis situations.

Chapter 4 explores another primary area of focus for IR scholarship: development and humanitarianism. The chapter argues that utilising a critical intersectional framework enables us to more effectively examine religion's entanglement with diverse development and humanitarian issues, make sense of the diversity and complexity within this sector, and identify possibilities for partnership and engagement that may otherwise have been missed. The chapter also highlights the mistakes that can occur in development when researchers and policymakers either fail to consider religion at all or only adopt a reductionist simplistic approach to how it manifests. Yet addressing these shortcomings cannot be separated from the need to also address the underlying power inequalities on which the development and humanitarianism sector is based, inequalities that are also entangled with secularist logic. A move away from notions of "development" towards partnership, cooperation, and mutual learning would facilitate greater ownership by local communities, as well as remind donor governments and agencies that those problems we currently label as "development" are in fact global challenges for all communities everywhere.

Chapter 5 examines religion's intersection with human rights, law, and public life. It focuses on four key issues, namely, the right to freedom of religion or belief, minority rights, indigenous rights, and the regulation of religion in the secular public sphere. The chapter demonstrates that interpretations of "religion" in law and human rights policy and practice often reflect broader power inequalities between majority and minority communities, and between states and individuals. The majority understanding of what "religion" is informs decisions that are made regarding what does and does not count as religion and the best ways to uphold and protect the rights, dignity, and freedom of diverse groups and individuals around the world. Yet the application of this "majority understanding" often results in contradictory outcomes, with little regard for contextual specifics and nuances, or for the perspectives and aspirations of the communities themselves. A critical approach invites us to acknowledge the inequalities embedded in human rights discourses and institutions and the legacies from the colonial era that shape the interpretation and application of law regarding religion, which then in turn facilitates research, policy, and practice that more accurately reflects the perspectives of the individuals and communities concerned and the realities on the ground.

*Unlearning Religion as (We Think) We Know It*   17

Throughout the book, in addition to the research of other scholars, I draw on my own fieldwork experiences from several different contexts. I also reflect on my own interactions with policymakers, defence force personnel, and civil society practitioners to inform the research framework that I propose here.

At its core, the main goal of the book is to disrupt the idea that "religion" is an object of and for analysis. "Religion" is not a pre-existing, static, unchanging, clearly definable entity: it is an idea, a social and cultural phenomenon, constantly evolving, never the same from one place and time to the next. Weaning ourselves off the idea that "religion" can be clearly defined, described, identified, and analysed and appreciating the dynamic nature of religion as both conceptual category and embodied, experienced practice will enable analysis of international politics that more comprehensively reflects the diversity and nuance of people's everyday lived realities.

## Notes

1  I am grateful to Judd Birdsall for drawing my attention to this fascinating tradition.
2  College voor de Rechten van de Mens, "Verbod gezichtsbedekkende kleding," August 1, 2019. Accessed on April 15, 2022. https://mensenrechten.nl/nl/toegelicht/verbod-gezichtsbedekkende-kleding.
3  France24, "French Move to Extend Ban on Religious Symbols Sparks Fears of 'Radical' Secularism." *France24*, October 30, 2019. Accessed on April 15, 2022. https://www.france24.com/en/20191030-french-move-to-extend-ban-on-wearing-religious-symbols-sparks-fears-of-radical-secularism.
4  Brems, Eva. "ECJ Headscarf Series (5): The Field in Which Achbita Will Land – A Brief Sketch of Headscarf Persecution in Belgium." *Strasbourg Observers*, September 16, 2016. Accessed on April 15, 2022. https://strasbourgobservers.com/2016/09/16/ecj-headscarf-series-5-the-field-in-which-achbita-will-land-a-brief-sketch-of-headscarf-persecution-in-belgium/.

# 2 Relearning Religion
## Connecting Theory with Practice

The identification and critique of different secularisms and their impact on the study of religion and International Relations (IR) is a crucial foundation of critical theoretical approaches. That secularism is no longer taken for granted as neutral, natural, and universal reasoning is due to the work of pioneering scholars in this field who drew on insights from religious studies and anthropology to highlight the secular conceit that inhibited IR researchers from appreciating the nuanced, dynamic, and varied ways this phenomenon we refer to as "religion" manifests in international politics and diplomacy.

While the critique of secularism arguably forms the pivotal moment in the emergence of the critical study of religion in IR, the question arises: what comes after that? Once the dominant framework has been deprived of its innocence and hegemony (Mahmood 2016), how then do we proceed to analyse religion from a "critical" perspective?

Stacey Gutkowski (2011, 611) notes in her groundbreaking study of the British secular security imaginary and its impact on the 2003 Iraq war that there were "certain ambivalences" towards engagement with and development of a better understanding of Islam. While recognising that the "Islam dynamic" was "vaguely important", British officials were unwilling to invest significant time and resources into fostering and enhancing expertise. This ambivalence, Gutkowski suggests, stems from the influence of two competing myths about religion – that religion is dangerous and that it is benign. Consequently, religion either is too volatile to risk encouraging through engagement or is not significant enough to bother with.

It is not only the British policy and military establishment who display such ambivalence. While "religion" in various forms has been back on domestic and foreign policy agendas for nearly two decades, the kind of ambivalence Gutkowski describes persists, with governments investing in deepening expertise in religion-specific areas such

DOI: 10.4324/9781003037057-2

*Relearning Religion: Connecting Theory with Practice* 19

as freedom of religion or belief (FoRB), but not in other portfolios. What explains this continued ambivalence in the face of mounting evidence of religion's significance in global politics? I would suggest that it is, in part, because despite growing awareness that the dominant secular lenses through which we have analysed and carried out international affairs are inadequate for analysing religion, it is as yet unclear exactly how we should approach religion differently.

Arguably, the single most revolutionary insight to emerge from the critical study of religion in IR is that "religion" is not something that is clearly identifiable and definable, but rather operates as a shape-shifting category, meaning different things in different times and places, depending on who is using this category and what they are using it for. This insight departs sharply from more standard approaches that take the idea of religion as given. Rather than asking how important or significant religion is and what type of influence it exercises, critical analysis instead asks what "religion" means, who gets to decide, and what the consequences are of defining religion in one way and not another for law, policy, and daily lived realities of people and communities. This shift changes the way in which we identify issues and dilemmas where "religion" is present, the research questions that we formulate to explore and make sense of those dilemmas, and the theoretical and methodological frameworks through which we go about discovering answers to those questions.

In this chapter, I present a basic outline of critical intersectional approaches to studying religion in IR. It is basic because, as with all critical approaches, the possibilities available for exploring these issues expand exponentially through creative transdisciplinary collaborations. As Jenny Edkins (2019) notes, part of what makes critical approaches to IR in general so exciting and fascinating is that they are rapidly evolving, but this also makes them difficult to comprehensively encapsulate. The critical study of religion is no different. Much of the most innovative work in this field has been done through combining IR's focus on power and the role of states and the states-system, including international law, with a "lived religion" approach that considers how these structures and forces impact everyday lived realities of people on the ground. On the one hand, this means that critical approaches are more expansive in that they draw on a broad array of disciplinary, theoretical, and methodological inspiration. On the other, it means that critical approaches are narrower in scope, since they emphasise the importance of contextual specificity and embeddedness, to understand how people and communities are affected.

## 20 *Relearning Religion: Connecting Theory with Practice*

The chapter outlines what I suggest are three primary considerations when thinking about how to critically analyse "religion" in IR. The first consideration is that we must begin our examination of "religion" in IR by focusing first on the specific context we are interested in. Second, we must explore "religion's" entanglements with other dimensions traditionally ignored by mainstream IR analysis, including race, gender, class, and environment, amongst others. In other words, critical approaches do not begin with a priori assumptions about *whether* religion matters or not but seek to explore both *what* "religion" actually is and *how* it matters, for whom, and why, depending on the specific context. This could be termed a "right-sizing" (Mandaville 2021) approach to the study of religion, though such a term should be used cautiously, in order not to imply that there is in fact a right way or right level of emphasis to give to religion in analyses of world politics. Rather, "right-sizing religion" describes an approach that moves away from the predominant tendencies to either "over-" or "under-emphasise" the significance of religion.

The third consideration is how we unpack what "religion" itself actually is. Since critical approaches are concerned with how "religion" is understood by different actors in diverse contexts, this does not entail developing a specific definition of "religion". In any event, as religious studies scholars have known for some time, it is impossible to arrive at a definition of religion that has widespread agreement and acceptance. Rather, for scholars interested in a critical understanding of religion's place in global politics, it is important to be specific and precise with reference to the particular context that is being researched. For example, if we are exploring the place of religion in international human rights law and advocacy (as we will consider in Chapter 5), it is not accurate enough to say that we are examining "religion". What exactly do we mean here? In the first instance it requires at a minimum being explicit about the specific religious tradition that we are examining. Often in contemporary IR, when we (scholars and policymakers) say "religion" what we are really referring to is "Christianity" and/or "Islam". Such terminological sloppiness renders our analysis imprecise, collapsing into generalisations that do not make sense in all contexts, and particularly not those contexts where Christianity or Islam are not part of the dominant meaning-making frameworks. Yet, in addition to being more precise about the religious traditions we are considering, I further suggest that there are at least three sub-categories of dynamics related to the overarching category of "religion" that scholars and analysts can consider and select from to bring more precision to their research and policy. I have labelled these sub-categories as

*Relearning Religion: Connecting Theory with Practice* 21

actors, identities, and narratives. Each of these can be broken down still further to allow for even more specificity and precision in analysis.

One obvious question that arises is what the benefits are of critical analysis of religion in world politics when it becomes so focused on context and specifics. Is there not a risk that the findings of such studies become so particular that they cannot be generalised, expanded out, and applied to other areas and issues within IR? As a first response, both yes and no. Part of what I am suggesting in this book is that critical approaches to studying religion in IR contain a generalisable commitment to (1) destabilising secular assumptions that religion can be clearly identified and labelled; and (2) examining the various dimensions of the category of "religion" within their historical, cultural, political, geographic, and economic contexts and in their interrelationship and interconnectedness with other categories such as gender, race, class, and species. Yet the commitment to contextual specificity and embeddedness inevitably means that the findings of such studies are unlikely to be generalisable, though they may provide some signposts to guide the way and raise important questions to be asked in relation to other contexts and issues.

A second response, however, is why should the goal of our research be findings that are broadly generalisable? The urge to generalise the findings of research carried out within a very specific location risks perpetuating the kind of "epistemological violence" (de Sousa Santos 2014) on which the discipline of IR (and many other social science and humanities disciplines) is founded, namely the assumption that the secular Euro-American experience of politics, religion, and statehood represents the universal human experience, thereby silencing or erasing millions of unique, alternative perspectives, voices, and wisdom. By placing context at the centre of our research and paying attention to how religion interacts with global power structures and other categories of marginalisation and exclusion, critical scholars attempt to address these silences and uncover the specific experiences of the spiritual and psychological wounds inflicted by colonial practices, past and present (Ndlovu-Gatsheni 2015).

## Analysing Lived Religion and its Implications for World Politics

In this section, I outline in more detail the three key considerations I flagged in the introduction to this chapter that are crucial for connecting IR theorising on religion with the realities we encounter on the ground in practice. First, we must move away from the tendency to

## 22  *Relearning Religion: Connecting Theory with Practice*

begin with a fixed idea about "religion" and instead depart from the context that we are exploring and what religion means in that context. Context refers to the physical location and the relevant historical, cultural, political, economic, and other factors that make up the distinctive features and unique setting of a particular place. Yet context also refers to the specific policy or issue area that we are examining, since specific discourses and dynamics feature in relation to particular policy issues that may not be as relevant or present for other policy issues.

Second, we need to move to studying religion as an integrated, intersectional, contextually embedded, fluid, constantly shifting and evolving dynamic in world politics, rather than as a singular static, unchanging object. Third, we need to be much more precise regarding what we mean by "religion". Instead of speaking about "religion" in general terms, we need to be specific regarding the religious tradition that is salient to the topic, issue, or context under analysis, as well as more explicit about whether we are concerned with analysing the presence and influence of religious actors, identities, or narratives. The next three subsections unpack how we can apply each of these considerations in our analysis of religion and IR.

### *Contextually Embedded, Integrated, Intersectional Analysis of "Religion"*

Critical approaches to studying religion and IR attempt to overcome the dominant tendency to view religion as a realm of human activity that is somehow separate and different from other spheres. Rather than departing from unquestioned, taken-for-granted assumptions about what religion is and does, critical approaches aim to problematise those taken-for-granted assumptions, highlighting the possibility that these assumptions are not widely held and do not reflect the reality of lived experiences for diverse communities. Subsequently, critical studies of religion and IR seek to establish: (a) what the alternative ideas and assumptions about religion are that exist in specific contexts on particular issues; (b) how the category of religion takes on those different meanings for diverse actors in different contexts; and (c) what the consequences of those diverse meanings are for social structures, power relations, policy, law, and everyday lived realities.

Critical approaches to religion and IR therefore require an intersectional approach to religion as well as an intersectional understanding of context. Critical approaches dispense with the division between domestic and foreign affairs that shapes so much of IR analysis and policymaking. Instead, critical scholars recognise that what takes

## Relearning Religion: Connecting Theory with Practice    23

place within domestic state politics inevitably affects what occurs at the international level. Further, critical scholars pay attention to how global policy developments and discourses infiltrate domestic socio-political arrangements, conscious that concerted international efforts to address certain shared policy and security concerns will inevitably impact social and political relationships on the ground. Such interconnections and repercussions are unavoidable in a globally interconnected and integrated world, yet much of mainstream IR analysis persists in only or primarily focusing on what occurs between states in the international environment. An obvious example of these dynamics are global efforts under the umbrella of "countering violent extremism" (CVE), a discourse that has diverse yet clear consequences for different religious communities and minorities across the world, consequences that critical scholars of religion and IR have identified and highlighted. This research will be discussed further in Chapter 3.

Critical approaches to religion share core theoretical assumptions with other critical IR approaches. First, while the state may still be the primary actor in global politics, it is by no means the only actor shaping and shaped by global political developments. Second, while the international system may be the primary sphere in which the state implements its foreign policy, it is not the only arena in which the consequences of states' foreign policy is observable and consequential.

This leads to an understanding of context that is focused on both geography and discourse. The consequences of global political developments will play out differently depending on the specific national context in which they are observed because of unique local histories, cultures, politics, economics, environments, and religions. Yet also, the context of a research project is shaped by the specific discourses and grammars of the issue being investigated. For example, the dynamics around religion and international security issues such as conflict, terrorism, and CVE will be unique from, albeit related to, the dynamics surrounding religion and international humanitarianism and development. In paying attention to context, critical researchers must be aware of these two components – the space and place-based elements and the linguistic and discursive elements of context.

Identifying and articulating these characteristics of the context (see Figure 2.1) is thus the first step in defining the parameters for a contextually embedded critical analysis of religion and IR.

Following this, the next part of the process is to consider the place of "religion" within that context. Notice that I am using the term "place" rather than "role". This is a conscious and specific linguistic choice as part of an effort to move our thinking away from the idea

24  *Relearning Religion: Connecting Theory with Practice*

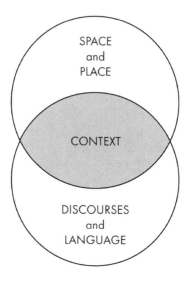

*Figure 2.1* Visualising Context: Space, Place, Discourses, and Language combined.
Image Credit: Jessica Mills Designs.

that "religion" as such has agency. Focusing on the place of religion rather than the role of religion also helps orient our thinking to consider the relationships and interconnections between the category of religion and the other elements of the context under investigation.

As we observed in Chapter 1, a prevailing tendency in IR approaches to studying religion is to either over- or under-emphasise religion's place and significance. In contrast, critical approaches seek to integrate attention for religion alongside other dimensions present within and relevant to a specific context and issue, including political frameworks, economic structures, gender identities and dynamics, inequalities of power resulting from historical and colonial processes, climatic and environmental factors, culture and tradition, and anything else that emerges as relevant as part of the contextual analysis. Figure 2.2 attempts to represent visually what this looks like conceptually – rather messy and complicated, which, after all, is often how things look in lived reality.

It is important to emphasise that not all factors will be equally important to studies of specific issues. This, again, is why consideration of both space and place and language and discursive context is so crucial. There will be places and times and issues where the category of

# Relearning Religion: Connecting Theory with Practice 25

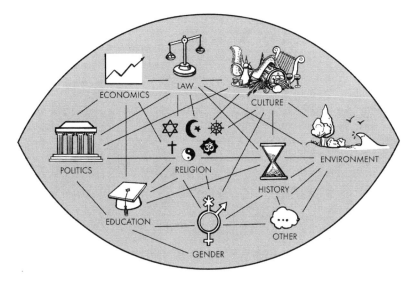

*Figure 2.2* Intersectional understanding of Context.
Image Credit: Jessica Mills Designs.

religion is central to explaining why a particular situation has arisen, others where religion is an important part of the mix, but not the only or even the primary factor to observe – for example, the 2021 coup in Myanmar (Frydenlund et al. 2021) or the 2022 war between Russia and Ukraine (Mandaville 2022) – and others where religion is indeed marginal to understanding the power relationships and dynamics at play. What matters here is that the significance of religion with reference to a particular issue and context has been established as a part of the analysis, not assumed prior to the analysis taking place, based on a priori assumptions about what "religion" is.

## Unpacking "Religion"

Whilst critical approaches eschew the idea that there is such a thing as "religion" that exists as an observable object or fact, they nonetheless are concerned with assumptions about what "religion" is and does that shape and are shaped by the particularities of the contexts and topics under investigation (Asad 2003). Alongside expanded conceptualisations of context and intersectional analyses of religion, critical scholars are also concerned with the ways ideas about "religion"

26  *Relearning Religion: Connecting Theory with Practice*

manifest and are used, who they are used by, how religious identities are formed, shaped, negotiated, and disciplined, and how religious actors are identified. This requires moving beyond speaking merely of "religion" and being more precise about the various ways the category of "religion" is present, how it is understood and operationalised by different actors, and how it may be significant for analysing and understanding a specific topic, event, or issue.

Such identifications and articulations must always be done in negotiation with the particularities of the context. An important consideration to keep in mind is that the term "religion" may not even exist, make sense, or mean what it means to us as researchers or analysts in specific contexts (Grüll and Wilson 2018). We need to establish this through background and preliminary research and then determine what is the appropriate language to use.

At the same time, based on what we already know and understand of how "religion" plays out in diverse contexts in contemporary politics, it is possible, I suggest, to identify three sub-categories within "religion" that enable us to be more precise in our analysis. These are actors, identities, and narratives. I am not implying that these are the only sub-categories we should pay attention to, or that how I describe them below is in any way complete and comprehensive. I have undoubtedly missed important aspects, also because each context will reveal different significant elements of the category "religion" and thus also of these sub-categories. While I discuss each of these sub-categories separately, they are inevitably interconnected, entangled, and overlap at particular points and in specific contexts (see Figure 2.3). The overall argument remains the same, however – we need to be more precise and specific to context when we research and analyse religion as critical scholars of IR, all the while recognising the inevitable messiness and complexities of lived realities.

## Actors

The first of the three sub-categories I propose is "actors". Within this sub-category, it is important that the actors included either self-identify or are identified by others within the specific context as "religious", rather than that we as researchers ascribe these categories and labels from our own vantage point with its associated biases and assumptions. As part of that (self-)identification by actors within the context of focus, we can then also begin to unpack what assumptions about "religion" itself sit behind the application and use of these labels and terms.

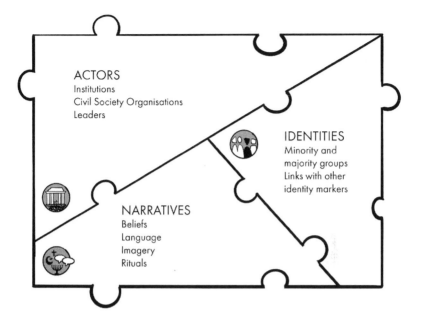

*Figure 2.3* Unpacking Religion: Actors, Identities, Narratives.
Image Credit: Jessica Mills Designs.

Some "religious" actors will be immediately obvious – these include official religious institutions and representative organisations such as churches, temples, mosques; civil society organisations that identify as faith-based; and individuals and/or groups who hold official leadership positions within religious organisations or institutions. Even with these obvious religious actors, it is important not to take for granted the meaning and authority these actors possess in specific contexts. Yet there are other actors that are less obvious, requiring a higher degree of precision in our analysis and descriptions or more in-depth investigation and analysis to determine exactly how such actors are "religious".

Consider, for example, former Australian Prime Minister Scott Morrison, who self-identifies as a Pentecostal Christian and who has openly discussed his faith and how it has shaped and influenced decisions made in relation to his political career in speeches to large audiences of fellow Pentecostals (Murphy 2021). Should we consider Morrison a political leader who is religious? A religious leader who is also a political leader? A religious leader because he is a political

## 28 *Relearning Religion: Connecting Theory with Practice*

leader who is religious? For different publics, each of these statements will be true and will also have different meanings and different implications. These different meanings will in turn have consequences for how we analyse and make sense of Morrison's leadership and policy-making, as well as how and why different communities respond to him in unique ways.

As part of investigating the role of religious actors in IR, we also need to pay attention to how we understand the category of religious "leader". In both scholarship and policy, there is a tendency to focus on the statements and actions of representatives of institutions that are officially recognised as "religious" by state and inter-governmental actors. Yet, institutionalised religion is only one way communities and groups centred around what we refer to as "religion" may be organised. Others are far more fluid and horizontal. Even within institutionalised religions, the official representatives are only one kind of "leader". Especially when researching religion in the context of humanitarianism and development, or gender equality and the rights of women and LGBTQI+ people, scholars highlight that it is often people at the grassroots who provide the most significant forms of leadership and change (Bartelink and Wilson 2020). Focusing on different kinds of leadership amongst religious actors is important to bear in mind for scholars, policymakers, and civil society actors when designing research projects, legislation and policy, or project interventions.

## Identities

Since the early 2000s, religious identity, as ascribed by both self and others, has become increasingly salient in the politics of migration and human rights. One obvious example of this is how immigrant communities in the Netherlands that had previously been described with reference to the national identity of their country of origin (e.g. "Moroccan", "Turkish", "Indonesian") were more and more referred to by their (assumed) religious identity as "Muslim" (Buijs 2009; Mepschen, Duyvendak and Tonkens 2010; Mudde 2019). In political commentaries and debates surrounding the so-called "refugee crisis" in Europe in 2015, people seeking asylum and protection in Europe were by and large assumed to be Muslim by the media, politicians, and the public because of their country of origin (which, for many displaced people during this crisis, was Syria) (Wilson and Mavelli 2016). Such assumptions serve to obscure the diversity within the global Muslim population as well the diverse religious genealogies that exist in countries such as Syria and others from the Middle East where

*Relearning Religion: Connecting Theory with Practice* 29

Islam is the majority but by no means the only religion, and where multiple kinds of Islam are practised (Eghdamian 2016; Zaman 2016).

Identities matter when researching IR because they provide the (self-) narrative in which certain behaviours and actions become consistent, permissible, and legitimate (Campbell 1998; Wilson 2012). In this way, they are also connected with, though distinct from, the sub-category of narratives, discussed below. When researching religion, paying attention to how "religious" identities are assumed, deployed, assigned, and interpreted and the consequences of that is crucial for understanding the power relations between different communities, how some practices are permissible, while others are not. The pertinence of such differences will be highlighted in the discussions in Chapter 5 concerning the *Dahlab v Switzerland* and *Lautsi and others v Italy* cases at the European Court of Human Rights.

An additional consideration is how religious identities map on to other pertinent markers of identity, such as gender, race, class, and nationality, amongst others. We can see these dynamics playing out in the ways "Muslim" identity has become increasingly entangled with categories of "refugee" and "terrorist" in the past two decades. The entanglement of these identities has enabled the increasing securitisation of migration and the criminalisation of both Islam and seeking asylum (Wilson and Mavelli 2016). What occurs here is the entanglement of religious and racial identities, so that people who look a certain way or come from a particular region of the world are automatically assumed to adhere to a specific set of beliefs, rituals, and practices. The Trump administration's notorious "Muslim ban" is one of the most obvious examples of this kind of overlapping and entanglement of identity politics. The significance of religio-racial identities of people seeking asylum is starkly observable if we compare the limited and exclusionary responses of countries to people fleeing Afghanistan after the Taliban takeover in August 2021 with the open and welcoming responses to people fleeing the war in Ukraine in March and April 2022 (Sajjad 2022). The struggles experienced by gay Muslim refugees, who are met with scepticism by refugee review tribunals because it is assumed that one cannot be both gay and Muslim, is another example of how both religious and sexual identities are proscribed based on prior assumptions that are not consistent with lived realities (McGuirk and Niedzwiecki 2016).

Critical scholars of religion and IR thus pay attention to which identities are pertinent in specific contexts on particular issues; how those identities are constructed and articulated; how different religious, racial, gendered, and class identities are entangled; who is constructing

30   *Relearning Religion: Connecting Theory with Practice*

and articulating those identities, to what purpose, and with what consequences; and how those identity constructions that are harmful could be or are being disrupted or challenged.

## Narratives

A third sub-category I propose that assists us in developing more precise analyses of the complex lived realities of religion and IR is "narratives". This analytical focus encompasses narratives that emanate from "religious" communities and actors as well as those narratives that are about "religion" or that borrow elements from what we understand as "religion", such as the "sacred", for example, as a category that cuts across multiple domains, including religion, nation, and family.

Within this sub-category, I suggest the inclusion of elements that have traditionally been assumed to be defining aspects of what religion is within secularist frameworks, such as beliefs and rituals, as well as other less obvious aspects, such as imagery, metaphors, language, and stories that permeate the "deep culture" (Galtung 1996) of different societies. Consistent with all research that focuses on narratives, analysing narratives in relation to religion and international politics is not only concerned with written and spoken language. It also considers non-verbal communication through images, gestures, and rituals, and how all these different modes of communication migrate across discursive contexts and the new meanings they bring with them or take on within each new context. An analysis of six State of the Union Addresses from different presidents from both the Republican and Democratic parties, from different moments in US political history, reveals how rituals, images, and metaphors migrate from the Christian, and particularly Protestant Christian, tradition across to the national discursive context of the US (Wilson 2012). This includes the unattributed use of Bible verses, the ritual of the State of the Union itself, national memorials, and remembrance days – what Bellah (2005) has referred to as "civil religion".

Analysis of such narrative elements matters for our understanding of religion's place in global politics because it can reveal unconscious or previously undetected ways in which meaning-making practices drawn from religious traditions may affect how different actors – religious or secular, state or non-state – make sense of and thereby respond to the world through policy and action.

## Conclusion

This chapter has presented an outline of preliminary considerations for how to research religion and IR from a critical perspective. Building on the critiques of secular-based approaches discussed in Chapter 1, the proposals in this chapter are a means through which to address and move beyond some of the identified limitations of secular-based approaches. They are not definitive or perfect, but they offer a point of departure for how we can be more nuanced and precise in research, policymaking, and practice when it comes to religion and global politics.

The chapters that form the remainder of this book apply the critical intersectional analytical principles and framework to three specific areas of IR research. Chapter 3 engages the topic often considered the "core business" of IR, that of conflict, security, and violence. Chapter 4 explores the place of religion in humanitarianism and development, while the final chapter considers human rights, international law, and public life.

# 3 The Things We Fear
## Religion in Conflict, Violence, and Security

A few years ago, I was invited to give one of two lectures on Religion and International Security for a defence training organisation. The brief I received informed me that the other speaker would be addressing "Islam", so it would be much appreciated if I could provide an overview of the main tenets of the other major world religions, whilst also highlighting the role that religion plays in conflict and extremism – and please keep to the time of 45 minutes.

This request and the division of labour in this session provide immediate insight into the underlying assumptions that inform the way many diplomats, policymakers, security analysts, and military personnel understand the category of religion and its relationship with conflict, violence, and security in the 21st century. The most obvious assumption is that Islam is the main religion of concern, since it is given the most time and attention. The second is that each religion contains a clear set of principles and guidelines that can be distinguished and itemised by external observers, without reference to the specifics and differences across cultural and political contexts. As we have established in the preceding chapters, there are significant problems with these assumptions that contribute to miscalculations and analytical errors. In the context of conflict and security, such missteps can be disastrous.

In this chapter, we will consider how to critically analyse the place of religion in conflict, violence, and security. The key step that such a shift requires is to move away from analysis that begins by focusing on religion's "role" in conflict or religion's relationship with violence. Such approaches begin from the assumption that "religion" is a distinct phenomenon that directly causes violence or facilitates peace. To develop critical approaches to the study of religion, conflict, violence, and security, we must begin with a focus on the context in which we are interested. We must first acquaint ourselves with the unique and

DOI: 10.4324/9781003037057-3

*Religion in Conflict, Violence, and Security* 33

specific historical, cultural, political, economic, environmental, and religious dynamics of each context. From there, we can consider how actors, identities, and narratives identified as religious in those settings contribute to meaning making and to structures of power, domination, violence, and exclusion.

In the 21st century, understanding and analysing conflict requires an acknowledgement that multiple different kinds of actors and phenomena instigate conflict, endanger the security of people and communities, and carry out violence (both direct, physical, and indirect, structural violence (Galtung 1969)). This chapter explores the place of religion not only in relation to so-called "regular" wars and conflicts but also in relation to "irregular" conflicts, violent insurrection, terrorism, and insecurity. It suggests that extremism and its prevention has become a central lens through which security is now conceptualised and enacted. As a result of this attention on extremism, religion has also become a more prominent feature of international security and foreign policy more generally, owing to the unbalanced focus on one particular kind of extremism – Islamist – of most intelligence and security analysis and strategy.

The chapter begins by highlighting the damaging consequences of secular assumptions in military policy and practice. The chapter explores how secular assumptions about religion have permeated and shaped dominant approaches to military strategy in contexts where religion is considered significant. I also examine approaches to violent extremism, an issue that has topped security policy agendas for over two decades. In both warfare and countering violent extremism (CVE), secular assumptions have contributed to severe misjudgements that have arguably destabilised precarious security situations, contributing to increasing insecurity, rather than reducing it.

The chapter then considers how a critical approach to analysing religion as outlined in Chapter 2 can assist us in arriving at more comprehensive analyses of conflict and security situations where religion is present. It explores the 2021 coup in Myanmar, the precarious security situation in Iraq after the 2003 war and the battle against ISIS, and the rise of right-wing extremism in Europe to demonstrate how a critical, intersectional approach can contribute to more effective analysis with longer-term consequences for establishing lasting peace and security.

## Secular Strategies of War

The political secularisms we explored in Chapter 1 have limited both research and practice on security, conflict, and violence in world

34  *Religion in Conflict, Violence, and Security*

politics. One of the clearest examples of this impact comes from Stacey Gutkowski's (2011, 2014) analysis of British involvement in the recent wars in Afghanistan and Iraq. Drawing on extensive interviews carried out with British defence force personnel, Gutkowski demonstrates that the tendency to treat "religion" as a singular, monolithic, homogenous entity that operates in the same way in all places at all times was central to British "secular ways of war". Initial engagements in Afghanistan and Iraq drew on both the history of British colonial rule in the region and experiences in Northern Ireland during "the Troubles", all set against the backdrop of assumptions about the 16th- and 17th-century so-called "wars of religion" that are central to foundational myths of the modern secular state and states-system. Colonial era Orientalist attitudes towards the Middle East spilled over into 21st-century warfare, with the religious "Other" treated as pre-modern, strange, violent, irrational, and "ungovernable" (Gutkowski 2014, 103–104). This attitude was combined with another that developed during experiences in Northern Ireland, that religion was essentially a distraction from the main political and strategic goals of nationhood and independence (Gutkowski 2014, 69–73). Together, these prior assumptions led strategists and analysts to initially overlook the importance of religion in both Afghanistan and Iraq. The core underlying assumption that religion is somehow a separate distinct entity and realm of human activity also meant that British defence force personnel were unable to appreciate that religion and politics are inextricably entangled in Iraq and Afghanistan, as well as in many other parts of the world. The distinction between what is "religious" and what is "political" does not always make sense outside of Euro-American contexts (arguably even in European and American contexts this distinction is analytically unhelpful and does not reflect realities on the ground).

These insights reveal a complex relationship between ideas of secularism and security operating in contemporary international politics. Luca Mavelli (2011) argues that a mutually reinforcing relationship between security and secularisation exists at the heart of the modern state and thus is central to the study of war, military strategy, security, and IR more generally. "By establishing a connection between religion in its public and political manifestations and violence, these perspectives implicitly posit a positive relationship between security and secularization" (Mavelli 2011, 178). This positive relationship between secularisation and security rests on a fundamentally flawed understanding of religion and of European history and the emergence of the modern nation-state (Asad 2003; Mavelli 2011, 179). Rather than

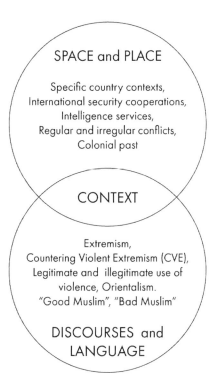

*Figure 3.1* The Context of Religion, Conflict, Security, and Violence.
Image Credit: Jessica Mills Designs.

resolving the problem of religious violence, this understanding of the relationship between secularism and security in some respects generates fear and insecurity. This is not accidental. The raison d'etre of the modern nation-state is to provide security for its citizens. This role of providing protection and security from the things we fear is what endows the state with power and legitimacy in contemporary global politics. In recognising that contemporary accounts of security and the secular state rest on problematic and flawed understandings of religion, we can see that political secularisms also contribute to the production of fear and insecurity. Secularisms thereby create the very situation from which people must be protected (Mavelli 2011).

These underlying secular prejudices, identified by Hurd, Mavelli, and Gutkowski, among others, contributed to the emergence in the 2000s of the damaging "countering violent extremism" framework, a

36  *Religion in Conflict, Violence, and Security*

generic term covering policy initiatives and programmes that emerged in the wake of 9/11 as a response to the perceived rise in threats from terrorism (Wilson 2021). This approach is underpinned by the pervasive assumption that a unique relationship exists between violent extremism, "religion" in general, and Islam in particular (also influenced by the Clash of Civilisations theory discussed in Chapter 1 (Suleman 2018). This assumption led to the development and implementation of domestic policies that targeted Muslim minorities in Euro-American contexts and foreign policies aimed at Muslim-majority countries, endeavouring to intervene in both cases to prevent the rise of extremism (Brown 2020). Yet these initiatives failed to recognise that (a) individuals who engage in extremist causes and behaviours do so out of a myriad of entangled factors and reasons; and (b) such policy interventions played into and reinforced existing narratives of "Western" domination that many Muslim extremist organisations promoted, perpetuating a self-fulfilling prophecy (Suleman 2018).

The failure to recognise other factors such as poverty, generational disempowerment and exclusion, psychological contributors, gender dynamics – what might be termed "secular factors" – amongst others, as significant in the development of extremist behaviours and tendencies contributed to a failure to heed the warnings of rising forms of other kinds of extremism, including right-wing, white nationalist, and "incel" (involuntarily celibate) extremism. These forms of extremism, which often, though not always, overlap, have had dramatic impacts on society and democracy in Europe, North America, Australia, and New Zealand in recent years, including the 2016 murder of Labour MP Jo Cox in the UK, the 2018 Toronto van attack, the 2019 attack on the Christchurch Mosque in New Zealand, and the 2021 attack on the US capitol building, all examples of violent acts motivated by these kinds of extremist ideologies. Further, these forms of far-right, white nationalist extremism have in many ways been fuelled by the almost obsessive focus on Islamist extremism in security policy, domestic and foreign, an obsession that essentially served to "crowd out" any attention for other kinds of violent extremism from the security agenda (Stevenson 2019).

So how do we avoid making such severe mistakes going forward? The remainder of this chapter focuses on developing the model outlined in Chapter 2 with specific reference to three ongoing situations of violence and insecurity: Myanmar, in particular the February 2021 military coup, the delicate political and security situation in Iraq, and the rise of transnational far-right extremism. There are any number of situations in the world that could be considered here – Indonesia,

*Religion in Conflict, Violence, and Security*   37

Afghanistan, Syria, Nigeria, Kenya, Mali, the US, Ukraine – the list goes on. I have selected these three cases, first, because they offer perspectives from diverse political, cultural, historical, religious, and geographic locations. Second, they are all long-standing seemingly intractable situations of conflict and insecurity (though, again, there are any number of other places in the world that could be described in similar ways). Third, dominant narratives about these environments give varying degrees of attention and emphasis to the role of religious actors, identities, and narratives, at times too much and at others too little. Further, there is a tendency within IR and dominant media and political discourses more generally to focus on locations at the periphery of global power, reinforcing the idea that conflict and insecurity are issues that emanate from and only matter "over there", away from the centres of global political power. It also subtly reiterates these power imbalances by replicating the assumptions of secular modernist discourses, that conflict, violence, and security are primarily concerns in less developed contexts, where irrational, chaotic "religion" has not yet been tamed and brought under the control of the rational, orderly "secular". Recent developments in Europe, North America, Australia, New Zealand, and elsewhere make clear that this is not the case. The US is often examined here as something of an aberration, yet there is clear evidence that far-right extremism, violence, and insecurity is a phenomenon that should be of growing concern in multiple locations around the world. Consequently, I include a discussion of Euro-American contexts here as a small contribution towards addressing this imbalance.

Despite the immense diversity across these three cases, there is an important element that connects them – the impact of narratives about violent, radical, extreme Islam circulating in global policy and media discourses. "Extremism" has come to permeate and dominate paradigms and approaches to international conflict and security, especially where "religion" is (seen to be) involved. The preoccupation bordering on obsession with Islamist extremism that followed the events of September 11, 2001, had four major consequences regarding broad understandings of religion in diplomacy, foreign policy, and security thinking. First, it built on and reinforced pre-existing narratives and assumptions about both "religion" and "Islam", and their relationship to violence, chaos, and irrationality, premised largely on shallow, superficial understandings of both "religion" and "Islam". Related to this, "extremism" was treated as something different, special, exceptional, unknown, similar to the way "religion" had been analysed up to that point. This approach failed to recognise that the causes

## 38  *Religion in Conflict, Violence, and Security*

of extremism are often similar to the causes of other anti-social behaviours such as alcoholism, addiction, and petty criminality (Wilson 2021). Second, the preoccupation with Islamist extremism spawned new modes of thinking and operating in world politics, where "extremism" became the number one security concern, as well as being the discursive device through which governments classified actors who challenged the authority of the state. Third, it reinforced an existing tendency to ignore the cultural, political, historical, and religious specificities of different locations, erasing the substantial diversity across locations within regions as varied as the Middle East, North Africa, South Asia, Central Asia, Sub-Saharan Africa, and Europe and combining them into a singular globalised threat of violent Islam (Jones and Smith 2005; Gutkowski 2014, 101–102). Further, "religion", "Islam", and the people, communities, and cultures in these regions are often viewed as "frozen in time", primordial, pre-modern, static, and unchanging, described through Orientalist tropes from the 19th century (Said 1978; Fowler 2007). Fourth, the preoccupation with Islamist extremism contributed to analytical missteps, resulting in a failure to identify threats from other kinds of extremism beyond Islamist and the complex interconnections between multiple kinds of extremism (such as "incel", anti-semitism, and far-right white nationalism), an error that we are only now beginning to address in broader analysis.

The goal of the discussion in this chapter is to demonstrate how giving consideration to religious actors, identities, and narratives, alongside of and in connection with other dynamics relevant to the specific contexts, contributes to enriching our understanding of specific conflict situations. This in turn creates more possibilities for addressing and pursuing mediation and conflict transformation. Religion is not the silver bullet that explains everything, but neither is it utterly irrelevant. Appreciating the unique dynamics associated with religious actors, identities, and narratives in each context enables us to develop fuller, more comprehensive analysis and in turn more effective policy responses.

Since the context and the sub-categories of religion look different for each case, the chapter applies the critical framework to each case individually, although there are some shared contextual features and types of actors, identities, and narratives across the three cases, as Figures 3.1 and 3.2 reminds us.

It needs to be stressed that these short overviews give only an introduction to what critical intersectional analyses might look like. Each of these contexts is immensely complicated and providing a full, complete impression of their dynamics in this short chapter is impossible. The goal is rather to provide a brief insight to what critical approaches

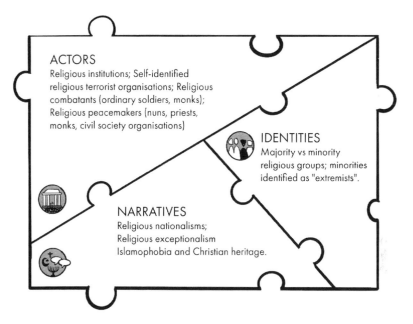

*Figure 3.2* Religious Actors, Identities, and Narratives in conflict and security.
Image Credit: Jessica Mills Designs.

to religion and IR can help us to uncover, with the caveat that there is far more to each of these conflict situations.

## The 2021 Military Coup in Myanmar

In the early hours of 1 February 2021, key figures in Myanmar's National League for Democracy (NLD) party, the party that had won the November 2020 elections in a landslide, were detained by the Tatmadaw (Myanmar's military), under the command of General Min Aung Hlaing (Charney 2021). This included state counsellor and popular political figure Aung San Suu Kyi. The Tatmadaw justified this manoeuvre by citing the constitutional provision that allowed the army to take control during national emergencies. What was the "national emergency" that prompted the coup? According to the Tatmadaw, alleged incidents of fraud had taken place during the November 2020 elections, which rendered the NLD's victory null and void, despite the National Election Commission having initially found no evidence of

40    *Religion in Conflict, Violence, and Security*

such fraud (Cuddy 2021). The coup is just one of the more recent incidents in the decades-long power struggle taking place between the Tatmadaw and Aung San Suu Kyi and the NLD.

In the context of an event as dramatic as a military coup, it is easy to overlook other dynamics contributing to the political unrest and instability in Myanmar. That the struggle is primarily about democratic governance of Myanmar needs to be emphasised. However, just below the surface of this struggle for democracy are myriad other tensions that need to be addressed and resolved for lasting peace and democratic reform in Myanmar to be achieved (Hayward and Frydenlund 2019). These tensions revolve primarily around what Myanmar democracy will look like and, crucially, who it will be for, and who will be allowed to participate as fully fledged enfranchised members of the Myanmar polity. At the heart of these tensions are complex issues connected to colonial history, political and economic inequality, diverse ethno-religious communities, and national identity. It is impossible to develop comprehensive, nuanced understandings of what is happening in Myanmar and what needs to happen for the future stability and democratic flourishing of the country without taking all these dynamics into account.

Following the framework developed in Chapter 2, this analysis considers the place of religion in Myanmar, in the context of other factors such as history, politics, and national identity, and pays attention to religious actors, identities, and narratives. Brief as this discussion is, it points to the complexity of the Myanmar context, as well as the richness and nuance that is possible through adopting critical approaches to analysing religion's place in conflict, violence, and security. It is important not to overstate religion's significance (Frydenlund et al. 2021) – religion is not the primary reason for the ongoing conflict and political instability in Myanmar or for the 2021 coup. At the same time, paying attention to religious actors, identities, and narratives and how they are entangled with other factors, including national identity, political inequality, and colonial history, provides a richer appreciation and understanding for the internal dynamics of the situation.

### *Colonial Burma and the Rise of Buddhist Nationalism (Context)*

Buddhist nationalism in Myanmar initially emerged during the 19th century when Myanmar (then Burma) came under the control of the British Empire. As a result of the mercenary aspirations of the British East India Company and the three Anglo-Burmese wars fought

*Religion in Conflict, Violence, and Security* 41

between the Burmese Army and British Expeditionary Forces, Burma was incorporated into what was then known as British India (Akins 2018). The King of Burma went into exile, and the British completely restructured local socio-political ethnic and racial hierarchies in Burma, primarily in order to best extract profit (Myint-U 2019). British authorities marginalised the Burmese population from public and military service, favouring participation by ethnic minority groups instead. This fuelled the resentment of the Burmese majority (Akins 2018). These policies created a fertile situation for the emergence of Burmese Buddhist nationalism as an anti-Indian response and later as part of the anti-colonial struggle against the British (Foxeus 2019). It was also central to reclaiming Myanmar identity after colonisation had ended (Myint-U 2019). Consequently, Buddhist nationalism in Myanmar is associated with the country's independence and freedom from colonial rule – its national pride (Foxeus 2019), an aspect that is not always understood by other religio-political groups (Myint-U 2019). Understanding this background is crucial for appreciating the significance of claims that have been made by both Suu Kyi and Hlaing to be the protector of Buddhism in Myanmar. These claims are shaped by and form part of a broader narrative around protecting Myanmar's heritage and promoting its interests and honour into the future, but also defending and protecting the way of the Buddha. Being the "true" leader of Myanmar is informed by ideals drawn from Kingship in Theravada Buddhism (Frydenlund et al. 2021). Thus, nationalism and religion cannot be easily separated in the Myanmar context.

At the same time, the idea that Myanmar is reclaiming its identity through Buddhist nationalism after colonisation is somewhat problematic. The territory covered by modern-day Myanmar had never been a united state prior to colonisation (Myint-U 2019). The Buddhist nationalism promoted in the country, like so many other nationalisms, is something of a historical myth. It glosses over the ethnic diversity, tensions, and inequalities that existed prior to colonisation and that continue to exist after independence. While in theory all 135 ethnic groups have equal participation, the reality is that the Burman majority retains dominance (Foxeus 2019, 669). Further, almost all the non-Burman minorities practise religions other than Buddhism (Hayward and Frydenlund 2019). As such, the rich ethnic and religious diversity of the country is largely not accommodated by the idea of Buddhist nationalism, thereby contributing to tensions amongst the different ethnic and religious groups.

The tensions between the Rohingya minority and the Burmese Buddhist majority stem back to British colonial rule. British colonisation, its

42  *Religion in Conflict, Violence, and Security*

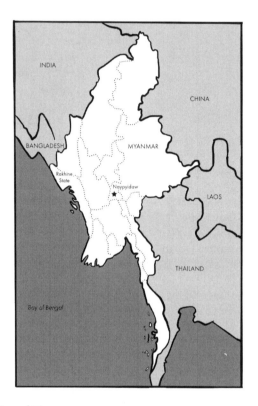

*Figure 3.3* Map of Myanmar.
Image Credit: Jessica Mills Designs.

facilitation of Indian migration to the region of modern-day Myanmar, privileging of Indian workers over Burmese, and granting independence to India before Myanmar (Foxeus 2019), all contributed to the emergence of anti-Indian sentiment which then feeds into the discrimination and violence experienced by the Rohingya minority in Rakhine state today (see Figure 3.3). As Foxeus (2019) notes, beginning in the 1990s, this anti-Indian sentiment slowly morphed into anti-Muslim sentiment, fuelled by the rising global fear of militant Islamist extremism.

This is not to say that religion as the point of distinction between the Burman Buddhist majority and the Rohingya Muslim minority had never been there prior to the 1990s. Rather, it is to highlight that where the ethnic/national dimension had been the primary focus before the 1990s, religion became the primary focus of the distinction from the 1990s onwards. This shift is important to note, since it demonstrates the fluid boundaries between categories of "religious", "ethnic" and "national" identities, as well as reminding us of how the political discourses and trends instigated by those at the centre of global power structures (in this case, particularly the US and its allies in the so-called "Global War on Terror") are discursively dispersed, with dire consequences for the lives of people at the margins (in this case, the Rohingya).

## *Unpacking Religion*

### *Actors*

Religious actors play an important role in promoting Buddhist nationalism in Myanmar amongst the general population as well as through lobbying activities and vocal support for pro-Buddhist laws and parties in Myanmar politics. Since the 2012–2015 period of violence between the Rohingya Muslim minority and the Burman Buddhist majority, two Buddhist monk-initiated movements have been especially significant – the 969 movement and the Organization for the Protection of Race/Nation and Religion, more commonly known by the abbreviation "MaBaTha" (Foxeus 2019). While religion and politics are formally separated by the constitution, and monks and nuns are disenfranchised and unable to vote, this separation is seen as protection of the *sangha* (monastic community) and Buddhism more generally from political interference, preventing it from being sullied by political conflicts and machinations (Hayward and Frydenlund 2019). Yet this separation does not prevent religious actors from mobilising and attempting to influence politics to protect and defend the Buddha's dispensation (teachings), though it does expose those monks and nuns who do get involved in such activities to criticism (Hayward and Frydenlund 2019). The MaBaTha formally supported the military-backed Union Solidarity and Development Party (USDP) in the 2015 elections against the NLD, accusing the NLD and Aung San Suu Kyi of being pro-Muslim (Hayward and Frydenlund 2019).

While the 969 and MaBaTha movements are crucial actors in politics and civil society promoting narratives of Buddhist nationalism and the role of the state in protecting Buddhism, other religious actors also play important roles in shaping alternative articulations of Myanmar identity that are more inclusive of ethno-religious minorities. With the opening up of civic space in 2011, significant interfaith initiatives have emerged within civil society movements in Myanmar that attempt to bridge tensions and divisions between different communities through organising shared events and activities (Hayward and Frydenlund

# 44 *Religion in Conflict, Violence, and Security*

2019). These actors, such as Religions for Peace Myanmar, and the activities and statements they organise and deploy provide an important antidote to the anti-Muslim rhetoric of Buddhist nationalist political leaders in the Tatmadaw, the MaBaTha, and the NLD.

*Identities*

In popular reporting on politics in Myanmar, the prominence of religion in general, and Buddhism in particular, is not often addressed. Even in reporting on the persecution of the Rohingya, the emphasis has often been on the religious (Muslim) identity of the Rohingya, not on the arguably equally significant religious (Buddhist) identity of the members of the Tatmadaw. Yet Buddhism occupies a central place in discussions about Myanmar's national identity. Whilst not officially named as the state religion, Buddhism is granted special status by the constitution in comparison with the other religions recognised therein (Christianity, Islam, Hinduism, and Animism) (Hayward and Frydenlund 2019). Both Aung San Suu Kyi and General Min Aung Hlaing have made claims to power through the mobilisation of the idea that they are the ultimate Buddhist leader, capable of protecting Myanmar as a Buddhist nation and defending the Buddha's dispensation (Foxeus 2019; Hayward and Frydenlund 2019; Frydenlund et al. 2021). The pervasive influence of such ideas and the strong association of the state with the protection of Buddhism amongst the majority population may go some way to explaining Aung San Suu Kyi's failure to condemn the genocide carried out by the Tatmadaw against the Rohingya in 2017. After being accused of being too pro-Muslim by the MaBaTha in the lead-up to the 2015 election, Suu Kyi needed to assure the majority population that she was pro-Buddhism, at the expense of the vulnerable minority – and her international human rights reputation (Charney 2021). This incident also exposed the limitations of the NLD as the main pro-democracy movement in Myanmar – a movement committed to the idea of excluding "non-Burmese" people from Burmese democracy (Prasse-Freeman and Kabya 2021).

It may be tempting to interpret such claims made by Suu Kyi and Hlaing of being the ultimate Buddhist leader as textbook examples of the instrumentalisation of religion in the pursuit of a political agenda. Yet such an interpretation does not do justice to the complex history and role of Buddhist nationalism in the anti-colonial struggles and independence movements in the country, as highlighted previously in the discussion about context.

## Religion in Conflict, Violence, and Security 45

### Narratives

The violence carried out against the Rohingya in 2017 by the Tatmadaw – described by the Myanmar government as "clearance operations" and the UN as "genocide" – provides a clear example of how global narratives of extremism colour local and national security and violence in diverse parts of the world. The Tatmadaw justified its actions against the Rohingya as retaliation for attacks on police and security forces in Rakhine state carried out by the Arakan Rohingya Salvation Army (ARSA) (which they claimed were revenge for years of oppression and violence (Bakali and Wasty 2020, 244)). These attacks were labelled as "terrorism" by the Myanmar government (which, at that time, was a complex and uneasy construction between the Tatmadaw and the NLD) and ARSA were branded as "extremists". The distinction between ARSA as a specific group carrying out violence and the Rohingya minority in general, already blurred, became even more problematic with this label. The Tatmadaw's violence against the Rohingya became justified as part of the global fight against extremism (Ma et al. 2018).

Yet the 2021 coup carried out by the Tatmadaw may have inadvertently served to undermine this constructed divide between the Buddhist majority and non-Buddhist, especially Muslim, minority in Myanmar, and the narratives deployed to maintain it. The eruption of protests in the aftermath of the 2021 coup was characterised primarily by the diversity of people involved. This included representatives from diverse religious communities, including Hindus, Christians, Imams, and Rohingya, who previously have not been as visible during protests for fear of making themselves more of a target (Frydenlund et al. 2021). Several commentators have observed that one outcome of the 2021 coup is the generation of greater unity across ethno-religious divisions, with the army offering a focal point for shared enmity for the diverse communities (Frydenlund et al. 2021). Shifts in relations between the Buddhist majority and the Muslim minority have been observed in the aftermath of the coup (Prasse-Freeman and Kabya 2021). Thus, the ethno-religious divisions in the country are not intractable. The coup may have inadvertently pushed the pro-democracy movement to become more pluralist, more inclusive, and more unified, arguably making it stronger and therefore more dangerous to the Tatmadaw, and weakening the influence that narratives of extremism have in the Myanmar socio-political landscape.

### Conclusion

The situation in Myanmar is incredibly complex, as even this short exploration makes clear. While religious actors, identities, and narratives

46    *Religion in Conflict, Violence, and Security*

are not the main explanatory factors for the tensions and instability that exist, or for the 2021 coup, neither are they absent or wholly irrelevant. Indeed, there are aspects of Myanmar's colonial and postcolonial history that do not entirely make sense without attention to the relationship between religious and ethnic identities and the actors who (re)construct those identities through their political statements and actions.

## Post-Conflict Iraq

George W. Bush's now infamous declaration of "mission accomplished" following the deeply controversial 2003 Iraq war has rung increasingly hollow over the intervening years. The US-led conflict, while ending the almost 24-year dictatorship of Saddam Hussein, generated new kinds of problems, especially regarding relationships between religious actors and their role in Iraq's social and political life. In the wake of Hussein's downfall, a power vacuum emerged that contributed to increasing insecurity and instability in the country (Gutkowski 2011, 617). The rise of ISIS – both a result of and a contributing factor to deepening and lengthening this power vacuum and instability – induced the US and its allies to return their armed forces to the region in 2014 after their first withdrawal in 2011, to end the violent extremism that their actions in the country a decade earlier had, in part, fostered (Al-Marashi 2021, Alshamary 2021). Both the Trump and Biden administrations committed to withdrawing US troops from the country entirely. In December 2021, it was announced that while formal military combat involvement had ended, approximately 2,500 US military troops would remain on the ground, transitioning the mission to an advise and assist role (Arraf 2021).

The situation in the country remains precarious. Popular analyses of the socio-political situation in Iraq often focus on seemingly primordial tensions between ethno-religious groups as a key determining element in the ongoing insecurity, while others will emphasise the impact of the ill-advised US-led war as part of the broader Global War on Terror. Yet such analysis, focusing on one specific element, offers only partial explanations for the continuing tensions and divisions in the country.

Just as with the coup in Myanmar and the events leading up to it, religion is not the only or primary explanatory factor for ongoing insecurity and conflict in Iraq and its impact should not be overstated. Neither, however, should religion be ignored. In Iraq, the significance of religion is primarily observable in the influence of religious leaders

*Religion in Conflict, Violence, and Security* 47

and the socio-political importance of religious identity. Disagreements and conflicts over issues of doctrine, belief, or articles of faith matter, but they are inextricably entangled with questions of power and privilege, discrimination, marginalisation, and exclusion, all of which have been exacerbated by the actions and interventions of national political actors, the authoritarian Baathist regime, and colonial and foreign powers in Iraq's history. The different perceptions and relationships that diverse religious communities have of themselves and each other have been shaped by centuries of complex interactions, influenced by colonial interventions, Cold War power struggles, and rising fear of Islamist extremism. The broader global framework of CVE continues to shape the interventions and interactions within the country, including recent and ongoing efforts to foster social cohesion through, among other initiatives, promoting the right to freedom of religion or belief (FoRB) for all of Iraq's ethno-religious groups. As Hurd (2015) and Mahmood (2016) have pointed out, however, promoting FoRB as a method for reducing inter-religious conflict and tension can have the opposite effect. An emphasis on FoRB can foster heightened attention and sensitivity to religious identity, making religious minorities more of a target for violence, rather than less, something we will explore further in Chapter 5.

What the history of Iraq reveals, from as far back as the Roman Empire to the present day, is that politics, ethnicity, and religious identity have always been inextricably entangled (Simon and Tejirian 2004, 3). While one could, in theory, focus on only one of these aspects, without attention to the others, such an analysis would leave crucial elements of Iraq's history and contemporary socio-political arrangements unexplained. In this brief analysis, I focus on the factors surrounding the emergence of the modern Iraqi state from the late 19th century onwards.

### Geopolitics, Religion, and the Formation of Contemporary Iraq (Context)

As much as it is crucial to understand the specific dynamics at the local level that have shaped the situation in contemporary Iraq, the history of this territory cannot be properly understood without also situating it in the context of the broader Middle East and Euro-American policies towards this region in general. The territory that is today known as Iraq (see Figure 3.4) was, in the 19th century, the site of imperial conflict between the Ottoman, Persian, and British empires (Simon and Tejirian 2004, 8). These conflicts took place around the

## 48  Religion in Conflict, Violence, and Security

boundaries of the Ottoman provinces of Mosul, Basra, and Baghdad. In other words, these conflicts were primarily about territorial control rather than "religious" in nature. Diverse religious communities in what is now modern-day Iraq lived together peacefully (Simon and Tejirian 2004), yet primarily within the confines of the provinces. Under Ottoman rule, each province was largely separate and independent from the others. People in Mosul and Basra knew little about each other and less about people in Baghdad (Kirmanj 2013).

At the same time, Ottoman control over the three provinces contributed to Sunni Muslim dominance in the public sphere, a dominance that continued up until the US-led invasion in 2003. The Ottoman Empire was Sunni; therefore, under Ottoman rule the Sunni minority were empowered over the Shia majority. This dominance continued after the collapse of the Ottoman Empire with the establishment of the modern state of Iraq for primarily pragmatic reasons – "most Shia lacked relevant experience to secure positions in the new administration" (Wainscott 2019, 5). The most significant factors shaping the creation of the modern Iraqi state were largely driven by imperial concerns of the British and French during and immediately after World War I (Kirmanj 2013). Britain wanted to secure a ready supply of oil for its navy, which had recently switched to oil from coal. Both powers

*Figure 3.4* Map of Iraq.
Image Credit: Jessica Mills Designs.

*Religion in Conflict, Violence, and Security* 49

wanted to ensure the dismantling of the Ottoman Empire post-World War I to protect their imperial interests and aspirations in the Middle East. Arguably, little has changed regarding the motivations of imperial powers in the region in the intervening century.

## *Unpacking Religion*

### *Actors*

Secular biases, assumptions, and misreadings of religious dynamics in Iraq are by no means the singular, main, or primary cause of the policy and strategic failures and errors in the recent wars in Iraq. Multiple other factors also played a role. Yet simplistic, generalised, and reductionist understandings of religious actors, identities, and narratives were salient. Developing more nuanced and contextually grounded analyses of the religious landscape in Iraq is crucial for post-ISIS community rebuilding.

While the Ba'ath party under Saddam Hussein was nominally secular, Shia Muslims experienced significant persecution and were forbidden from participating in the party, which ensured continued dominance of the Sunni minority over the Shia majority (Wainscott 2019, 6). It is important to highlight, though, that the Ba'ath state persecuted both Sunni and Shia religious leaders who did not comply with and support the regime (Helfont 2018). This persecution and suppression of religious leaders and communities under Saddam Hussein pushed many into exile or simply silenced them, fuelling resentment that would contribute to the emergence of inter-religious divisions, conflict, and extremism after the regime's downfall in 2003 (Helfont 2018). At the same time, the Ba'ath party was conscious of the important place of religious institutions, leaders, and practices for the Iraqi population, and so it was careful to allow a degree of freedom for those religious leaders it deemed "trustworthy" and supportive of the regime (Helfont 2018). This contributed to the appearance of a relative degree of independence and freedom for religious actors in Iraq, an appearance that was misleading and contributed to errors and miscalculations by Coalition forces as part of the 2003 Iraq war (Gutkowski 2011, 2014; Helfont 2018).

These miscalculations also occurred in part because of secular assumptions about "religion" in general, and Islam in particular, that coloured Coalition approaches to the 2003 war. "(A)t the strategic policy level, the British had a particular blind spot for the dynamics of Islamism. This was contextualised by a general misreading of Iraqi

## 50 *Religion in Conflict, Violence, and Security*

society" (Gutkowski 2011, 601). This misreading of Iraqi society was facilitated by both a lack of information (Helfont 2018) and an attitude of neo-colonial arrogance that the former colonial powers did not need to understand contemporary socio-political life in Iraq (Gutkowski 2011). The result was that Coalition forces assumed Iraqi society to be quite secular. British armed forces, for example, based their policy, strategy, and expectations regarding the behaviour of religious actors in Iraq on British Christian secular experiences, which were fundamentally different from the context of Iraq (Gutkowski 2011). These differences are especially observable in relation to understandings of the nature of religious authority and the relationship between religious belief and political strategy.

In essence, Coalition forces assumed that religious authority in Iraq operated in similar ways to the authority of Christian and, to a lesser extent, Jewish leaders within Euro-American contexts – private, social influence on the individual lives of followers, within the boundaries established and policed by state authorities (Gutkowski 2011, 615).[1] Yet, religious authority both operates differently and has different sources in the Iraqi context. There is no one model or framework for understanding religious authority across Iraq as a whole (Wainscott 2019). Some religious authorities in Iraq, such as Grand Ayatollah al-Sistani, mostly refrain from commentary on state politics (Gutkowski 2011), with the consequence that when they do intervene, their pronouncements carry significant weight (Wainscott 2019). Others are extremely vocal in their opinions and critiques of both national and international governing forces (Gutkowski 2011; Wainscott 2019). Both types of engagement carry influence and authority with different parts of the Iraqi public (Wainscott 2019). The sources of authority for religious leaders also differ across communities, partially because of the public political role carved out for select religious leaders under the Saddam Hussein regime (Helfont 2018), partially owing to the persecution experienced by these figures and the different ways religious communities themselves understand the nature of authority – as inherited, as earned (through education, for example), or as bestowed by patrons (Wainscott 2019, 27–31).

The important role of religious actors in Iraqi politics and society became acutely visible following the fall of the Ba'athist regime. As Helfont (2018) demonstrates, contrary to prevailing assumptions amongst scholars and policymakers prior to the 2003 invasion, the religious space in Iraq was heavily controlled and policed by the Ba'athist regime. With this authoritarian structure removed, previously silenced religious leaders, including extremists from across the

*Religion in Conflict, Violence, and Security* 51

different religious communities in Iraq, were able to openly work and promote their views. This took place in a public environment where piety and religious authority had been actively promoted by the Baathist regime, and thus extremist actors were able to wield significant influence (Wainscott 2019, 8; see also Helfont 2018).

The increasing acknowledgement of the significance of women in religious leadership in Iraq is a particularly important development, yet they continue to be under-represented. Women tend to be prominent and influential at the local level, while national level leadership roles are predominantly male. This is an important insight for policymakers, civil society actors, and researchers when seeking to engage with "religious leaders". It is essential to go beyond dominant assumptions and gendered stereotypes regarding who is and is not a "religious leader" (Bartelink and Wilson 2020). Understanding local dynamics, who communities respect and why they respect them, is crucial as part of these efforts. Similarly, women and youth are recognised by Iraqis themselves, as well as international civil society and intergovernmental actors working in the country, as having an important role in reducing individuals' engagement with extremist organisations and behaviours (Wainscott 2019).

*Figure 3.5* Shia pilgrimage in Baghdad, Iraq, February 2022.
Source: Courtney Bonneau Photography.

## 52 *Religion in Conflict, Violence, and Security*

*Identities*

Shifts in relationships of power and privilege in Iraq after the invasion played a significant role in the emergence of insurgencies and conflicts between and within different communities. With the fall of Saddam Hussein's regime, the power relationships between the Sunni minority and Shia majority almost reversed. The Coalition Provisional authority in Iraq employed a policy of "de-Baathification" (Alshamary 2021). The consequences of this were that former Baath party members were removed from civil sector positions and forbidden from holding them in the future. This had a direct consequence on the Sunni minority, who had dominated political institutions and the armed forces since Ottoman times. Post-2003, rather than holding positions of authority and influence, they lost their jobs and often were not able to find work even outside of the public sector and the military (Wainscott 2019). This exclusion from Iraq's social and political life after the war is an important element in the rise of Sunni extremism in the country. It fed grievances within the Arab Sunni population, which contributed to the subsequent civil war and extremist insurgencies (Alshamary 2021, 498–499). Al-Marashi (2021) argues that the post-2003 restructuring of Iraq's security forces, a process that actively excluded Arab Sunnis, enabled the rise of ISIS and the emergence of Shia militant groups in response to ISIS. De-Baathification generated a perception that Shia Muslims were working in cooperation with the occupying forces, a perception that positioned Shia Muslims as collaborators with the imperial power, rather than proponents of an independent Iraq (Helfont 2018, 230–231). Prevented from becoming part of the post-Baathist Iraqi state, as well as excluded from economic opportunities, many Sunni Muslim leaders instead advocated for an autonomous region for the Sunnis (Wainscott 2019, 8). As other research on the sources of extremism has highlighted, socio-political marginalisation and exclusion from economic opportunities are often contributing factors to the creation of situations in which people turn to extremism (see, for example, Schmid 2013; Doosje et al. 2016; Selim 2016).

*Narratives*

Coalition forces predominantly understood religious beliefs and identities as marginal to the "real" political and economic issues in Iraq and could consequently be disregarded (Gutkowski 2011, 619). This perspective was, again, based on a misunderstanding of and/or lack of information about the history of religion under the Baath party, as well

*Religion in Conflict, Violence, and Security* 53

as the experiences of Coalition partners in their own societies and/or previous conflicts (Helfont 2018). For example, based on experiences in locations such as Northern Ireland, British and Coalition forces misjudged the salience of Shia Islam as a political force in post-war Iraqi politics. They assumed that Shia identity would be reasserted primarily as an overarching label for the largely secular political aspirations of the Shia community. They mostly ignored the possibility that Shia Islam was itself a resource that provided content and structure to the formation of the political community and new and emergent institutions and constellations of power (Gutkowski 2011, 616–617; see Figure 3.5 as an example of public expression of Shia Islam). As discussed in Chapter 1, dominant secular frameworks contribute to over- or under-emphasising the importance of religion. Religion is either central or peripheral to the motivations of political actors, and is either sincerely held or strategically instrumentalised. Such "all or nothing" approaches leave little room for the possibility that political actors may be both sincerely motivated by deeply held religious convictions and may also instrumentalise those convictions within the broader population for the pursuit of strategic political goals (Gutkowski 2011, 621).

The salience of media, both traditional and social, is also crucial for understanding the operation of religious narratives and religious actors in Iraq. Traditional media is organised around religious groups, with very little diversity on religious television channels (Wainscott 2019). Integrating television, radio, and newspaper content so that Iraqis are exposed to perspectives beyond those within their own religio-political community is an important part of building relationships and understanding across social and political divides, yet must be done carefully, sensitively, and gradually. Social media has also proved to be a powerful tool for communication across groups, but also as a method of recruitment for extremist organisations, such as ISIS (L. Wilson 2017), who adopted particularly diverse and sophisticated strategies. Consequently, effective peacebuilding in Iraq needs to navigate and engage the social media landscape in ways that are sensitive to the dynamics amongst religious actors, identities, and narratives.

*Conclusion*

As with the emergence of extremism anywhere, the factors contributing to its rise in Iraq are multiple, complex, and contextually specific. The emergence of ISIS in Iraq occurred because of both intra- and inter-religious conflicts (that were also complicated by socio-economic and political factors); long-standing historical grievances regarding

## 54 *Religion in Conflict, Violence, and Security*

the dominance of foreign powers over the country – indeed, ISIS explicitly rejected the borders imposed by the British and French powers in the Sykes-Picot agreement following World War I, refusing to be subjected to any colonial logic or construct (L. Wilson 2017, 1) – and perceptions that certain communities were collaborating with the invading forces; the collapse of the authoritarian structures that had previously kept extremist groups in check and the subsequent power vacuum; the exclusion of certain groups from socio-economic opportunities as well as poverty and a lack of employment opportunities in general. Interference from external groups in the country also needs to be acknowledged.

In the aftermath of the conflict with ISIS, scholars and analysts have noted significant changes in the Iraqi religious landscape. New tensions have emerged in the post-ISIS environment amongst minority communities as well as between Sunni and Shia. These tensions are again related to economic and political issues of access to aid and resources and inequality amongst the different communities (Wainscott 2019, 41). Here, "religion" is salient as a marker of identity, rather than around specific differences in articles of faith. Iraqis themselves observe that there seems to be a growing turn towards secularism and atheism in the country, especially amongst young people, despite the continuing controversial nature of non-belief (Wainscott 2019, 21). This is seen as a direct response to the damage done by both Sunni and Shia extremism in the country. In interviews, Iraqis point to the harm caused by ISIS and the intra- and inter-group tensions between different religions as a key reason why many are sceptical of the role of religious actors in national politics and national level post-ISIS reconciliation projects. Yet, they want to see local religious leaders involved in reconciliation projects in local communities (Wainscott 2019, 42). Promoting reconciliation amongst the different religious communities will be crucial for peacebuilding in the post-ISIS environment, as there is evidence of increasing isolationism and unwillingness to engage across religious identities (Wainscott 2019, 26).

The Iraq case demonstrates that assumptions about and perceptions of "religion" are as significant in conflict and security as local dynamics and relationships between actors on the ground (Gutkowski 2011, 596). Consequently, when analysing any conflict setting and when developing policy or strategy for engagement in conflicts where religious actors, identities, and narratives are salient, it is imperative that scholars, policymakers, analysts, and civil society actors critically interrogate their own assumptions about these phenomena. Such critical self-examination contributes to identifying potential blind spots

Religion in Conflict, Violence, and Security   55

about what "religion" is and does that can in turn open space for more nuanced analysis of religious dynamics within the context in question, not to mention alternative pathways for policy interventions and conflict transformation.

## The Transnational Rise of Far-Right Extremism

Since 2010, there has been a noted rise in transnational violence associated with and motivated by far-right extremism, generating greater urgency and attention for this issue on the security agenda of many states and inter-governmental organisations (Auger 2020). While a diversity of movements and ideologies are encapsulated within this broad terminology, they are loosely united via a focus on identity politics, in particular religio-racial identities, and the need to preserve or defend a threatened "in-group" against an enemy "out-group". Within far-right extremism, such in- and out-groups are formed through a focus on specific religious, racial, class, and/or political identity markers. Arguably, it is the increased attention for religious identity in the early 21st century that has both encouraged and characterised this era of far-right extremism, by comparison with its 20th-century variants. Examples of far-right terrorism include the Anders Breivik killings in Norway in 2011, the National Socialist Underground terror cell, the 2016 murder of British MP Jo Cox, the Toronto van attack in 2018, the 2019 attack on the Christchurch Mosque in New Zealand, and the 2021 attack on the US capitol building, with numerable other incidents occurring as well throughout the last decade (Koehler 2016).

Whether carried out by individuals acting alone or members of extremist organisations, these acts of violence share several key features, despite occurring across different contexts. Linked to and fuelled by far-right populist political ideologies and rhetoric (Blackbourn, McGarrity and Roach 2019), these kinds of extremist violence are characterised by a concern with protecting "the people" against a corrupt political and economic "elite" that threatens or has sacrificed national identity and pride for the sake of free trade that benefits only a few (Mudde 2019). A second, related characteristic is anti-immigrant and racist sentiment. Within this worldview, migrants are claimed to be "stealing jobs" from citizens at the same time as they are also supposedly living off the welfare of the state, which should be reserved for the benefit of (white) citizens. In the post-9/11 environment, anti-Muslim attitudes also form part of this anti-immigrant stance.

This third case is different from the previous two, in the sense that I do not focus on a specific geographic location. At first glance, this

56  *Religion in Conflict, Violence, and Security*

seems as though I am ignoring the specificities of context that I advocated for in Chapter 2, and there are undoubtedly unique contextually specific factors shaping the rise of far-right extremism in the UK that differ from those shaping the emergence of far-right extremism in the US, Germany, Australia, and elsewhere. Yet there is also clear indication and evidence that similar concerns and discourses shape far-right extremist activity across multiple contexts, with connections to religious dynamics, especially Islamophobia, cutting across geographic locations (see, for example, Ramos and Torres 2020; Knaus and McGowan 2021). As such, it is useful to consider this phenomenon in its transnational, rather than purely national, context.

### Defining the Far Right

In contemporary scholarship and public discourse, the term "far right" is commonly used to make a clear distinction between the extreme ends of the right-wing political ideological spectrum and more moderate centre-right positions. Mudde (2019) traces shifts in scholarly and policy terminology from the first decades after World War II, where "neo-fascism" was the main descriptor, driven by a concern with a repeat of the horrors witnessed in Europe under fascist regimes in the 1930s and 1940s. In the 1980s, the terminology moved to "extreme right", followed by "radical right" in the 1990s. In the early 2000s, "right-wing populism" was the term *du jour,* highlighting the linkages between the thin ideology of populism, with its focus on defending "the people" against the "corrupt elite", and right-wing political ideologies characterised by racism, anti-immigration, and rejection of (some aspects of) democracy. The shifts in terminology are reflective of changes in the phenomenon itself, changes in the broader sociopolitical domestic and global landscapes affecting policy priorities, as well as deepening of the scholarly understanding of the factors and circumstances contributing to the formation of right-wing extremist views and groups. I will here utilise the term "far-right" to be consistent with current scholarly approaches and thinking. As Mudde (2019) helpfully clarifies, populism is a feature of many, though not all, types of far-right extremism. Within the broader term "far right", he distinguishes between "extreme right", which rejects democracy, sovereignty, and majority rule, and therefore leans more towards authoritarianism rather than populism, and "radical right", which he argues does accept the essence of democracy, but rejects key features such as

*Religion in Conflict, Violence, and Security* 57

the rights of minorities and the rule of law. One of the most concerning developments in the rise of contemporary far-right extremism is that such views no longer represent the political fringe, but rather are present within governing coalitions, espoused by mainstream political parties, and accepted and repeated within segments of mainstream media (Mudde 2019; European Union 2021, 7–8).

The phenomenon of far-right extremism is highly complex and there is much debate in scholarly literature about how to define and make sense of it. It is anything but a coherent homogenous phenomenon. A recent European Union (2021) report highlights six main ideological threads within far-right groups and movements, many of which overlap and intersect, but are nonetheless distinct. These include neo-Nazi movements, anti-Islam and anti-immigration movements, (see, for example, Figure 3.6) identitarian movements, ultranationalist and neo-fascist movements, far-right sovereign citizen movements, and single-issue extremists, under which the report includes opposition to COVID-19 vaccination and other control measures, incel (involuntarily celibate) terrorism, and climate denialism (though this is less common in Europe than in other contexts such as Australia and the US). Intersections with conservative religious, particularly evangelical Christian, and political identities are also evident in relation to these single-issue extremist groups (Hoffarth and Hodson 2016; Veldman 2019).

Far-right movements and political parties themselves are not necessarily engaged in physical violence. Yet they advocate various forms of structural violence and perform discursive violence. Through their language and policies, they create an environment in which physical violence against minorities, immigrants, and people of colour becomes accepted and even viewed as an act of bravery or patriotism. The other crucial aspect that makes the rise of far-right extremism a security concern is that the anti-immigrant, anti-Muslim, anti-Semitic language and policies of the far right have become more common and more accepted within mainstream politics and media (Mudde 2019). While far-right extremist violence has its own unique flavours across different national and cultural contexts, within the broader shared cultural milieu of Europe and North America, there are commonalities. As a result of its focus on identity politics, far-right extremism is concerned with both domestic and international political and economic developments, meaning that it has local, context-specific manifestations, whilst sharing features with movements and phenomenon in other locations.

*Figure 3.6* Image from an anti-Islam protest, Poland, 2015.
Source: Silar, KORWiN.JPG, CC BY-SA 4.0.

## Unpacking Religion

### Actors

Although not the defining feature of far-right extremism, religious actors, identities, and narratives are entangled in this phenomenon in crucially important ways. These linkages have arguably become more acute within the last two decades, a consequence of the overriding focus on Islamist extremism and the rise in Islamophobia witnessed across Europe, North America, Australia, New Zealand, and numerous other contexts. Extreme right religious (usually Christian) groups often provide a support base for acts of violence, if not being explicitly involved in its execution. Similarly, perpetrators of such acts of violence often self-identify as religious (usually Christian), engaging in acts of violence against those who threaten the religio-racial identity and purity of the nation itself, most often Muslims and Jews (Auger 2020). The EU (2021) identifies anti-Islam and anti-immigration movements, identitarian, and ultranationalist movements as the types of far-right extremism where links with Christian religious identity and culture most prominently appear. Religious narratives, usually, though not always, entangled with right-wing populist rhetoric, contribute to creating an environment in which such acts of violence

*Religion in Conflict, Violence, and Security* 59

against non-white and non-Christian populations are legitimised and appear acceptable and even necessary in the face of a "threat" to the security of the nation (Stevenson 2019).

*Identities*

The religious identity of far-right groups has been emphasised more in response to the increased concern with Islamist violence and is in some respects a consequence of this phenomenon, rather than a precipitating factor. The far-right Austrian Freedom Party (Freiheitliche Partei Österreichs), for example, was strongly anti-clerical and anti-Catholic when it was first established in the 1950s, but since the 1990s has begun to describe itself as a defender of the Christian West against the threat of Islam (Hafez, Heinisch and Miklin 2019). As the religious identity of the "other" became more politically and discursively salient, far-right groups thus also asserted their own religious identity credentials to make the distinction and threat – and their role as defender of the faith – more obvious and acute.

*Narratives*

Arguably, narrative is the most salient of the three sub-categories of "religion" for understanding the entanglement of religious dynamics with far-right extremism. This is not to say that religious actors and identities are unimportant. Rather, the preponderance of public political narratives emphasising religious dimensions shaped the articulation of explicitly religious far-right identity politics and created the space for actors self-identifying as religious, specifically Christian (within Euro-American contexts), to openly associate themselves with far-right movements and sentiments (Esposito and Iner 2018; Esposito 2019).

Mudde (2019) argues that contemporary far-right extremism is a response to three "crises" (acknowledging the always political nature of whether something is labelled a crisis or not): the 9/11 terrorist attacks in the US; the Global Financial Crisis in 2008, and the so-called "refugee crisis" of 2015.[2] These events in combination generated the perfect conditions for a growth in far-right extremist groups, with the prevalence of security discourses and linkages with Islam and non-white minority groups as potential "threats"; devastating economic setbacks for white working-class communities; and the dramatic scale and speed of the ongoing displacement crisis (UNHCR 2022). Far-right extremists present themselves as defenders of the historical

## 60  *Religion in Conflict, Violence, and Security*

cultural legacy of the majority religion against the perceived threat from minority religious groups.

The impacts of these "crises" were not restricted to Europe and North America, however. India, for example, has experienced a rise in extremist far-right violence, linked with Hindu nationalism and anti-immigrant, and especially anti-Muslim, sentiment (Blackbourn, McGarrity and Roach 2019), entangled with the obsessive focus on Islamist extremism. A concern with jihadism has also featured as part of the justifications for violence against Rohingya people in Myanmar and Uyghur people in China. This is not to reduce far-right extremist violence to violence against Muslims. The phenomenon is far more complex than that and indeed cannot be understood solely as the result of populist political ideologies and rhetoric. Individual and socio-economic factors are also part of the complex mix of ingredients motivating and mobilising such acts. At the same time, however, it cannot be ignored that the global discourse emphasising Islamist extremism as the primary security threat in the 21st century has played an important enabling role in the rise of far-right, anti-immigrant, racist, anti-minority violence across diverse contexts (Esposito 2018; Esposito and Iner 2019; Mudde 2019).

*Conclusion*

This chapter has explored the place of religion in contemporary situations of conflict, violence, and insecurity across diverse contexts. It has demonstrated how the critical intersectional framework contributes to providing a more nuanced, detailed picture of where and how religion matters in contemporary international security, violence, and extremism.

What emerges from the three cases examined here is that the lens of extremism has come to dominate international security frameworks. This lens is intimately and inextricably entangled with the category of religion and all the problematic assumptions associated with it identified in Chapter 1. This obsession with religiously inflected extremism, specifically with "jihadism" or "Islamist extremism", has contributed to the emergence of other types of far-right, white nationalist anti-immigrant extremism through fostering Islamophobia. At the same time, in focusing almost exclusively on Islamist extremism, politicians, security analysts, scholars, and policymakers have overlooked far-right extremism as a security threat. Developing more nuanced, comprehensive analyses of religion and its relationship with violence and extremism can contribute to addressing this imbalance and neglect.

*Religion in Conflict, Violence, and Security* 61

The assumptions that shape analysis of religion in relation to violence and insecurity in the 21st century have also affected analysis, policy, and practice in areas of development, humanitarianism, and human rights, as we will explore in the coming two chapters.

## Notes

1 While this is a prominent assumption about how religious authority operates in Euro-American contexts, it does not always reflect reality. Religious leaders, such as the Pope, or various heads of evangelical movements in the US, enjoy a significant degree of public influence, in addition to their authority in the private sphere.
2 "So-called" because arguably this was a crisis of political leadership rather than a crisis brought on by people fleeing persecution and violence (Wilson and Mavelli 2016).

# 4 From Secular Development to Global Partnership

## Religion in International Aid and Humanitarianism

Several years ago, a colleague and I were approached by a faith-based organisation working in the development sector to carry out monitoring and evaluation of one of their projects. The goal of the project was to encourage shifts in attitudes amongst religious and community leaders on issues such as gender equality, child rights, healthcare, and good hygiene practices. It included workshops and conferences with these leaders in which religious teachings, sacred texts, rituals, beliefs, and other practices were engaged to offer a religiously grounded framework that facilitated action on these core development challenges. Employees of the organisation knew – from their own experiences, from the responses of participants, from feedback from the communities, from their own observations over the years – that the programme worked, across diverse contexts and with different religious traditions. Yet thus far, their own reports and findings had not been enough to convince potential secular donors and partners that this approach was effective in pursuing development goals. They concluded that the only way to provide convincing evidence to secular stakeholders would be through independent research carried out by external actors that demonstrated the "added value" of religion for achieving international development goals.

Our experience with this organisation echoed many of the observations and critiques that scholars have articulated in recent years about attitudes towards religion in the broader development and humanitarian sector. This faith-based agency was prompted to seek out external consultants to conduct monitoring and evaluation because their own internal reporting and evidence gathering was unable to convince other secular actors in the development sector of the importance of engaging with religion in the pursuit of development goals. This experience is indicative of the wider "secular bias" that scholars and practitioners have observed (Ager and Ager 2011; Wilkinson 2020).

DOI: 10.4324/9781003037057-4

*Religion in International Aid and Humanitarianism*   63

This "secular bias" translates as international development and humanitarianism being considered secular activities and religious actors as somehow distinct, separate, and their presence in international development and humanitarianism as suspect (Jones and Petersen 2011), an assumption grounded in a narrow, simplistic understanding of religion and embedded in broader secular paradigms.

A key outcome the organisation sought was evidence to demonstrate the "added value" of religion to development. This terminology highlights that development is seen primarily as a "secular" field of action. For religious actors to be taken seriously, they must prove that they bring something unique to the already existing terms and agenda of international development. Further, it shows that it is not only secular actors who promote such views. Religious actors also reinforce the dominant secular terms of the development sector. In other words, secularism provides the structuring logic for the development and humanitarianism sector. Ongoing barriers to engagement across religious and secular agencies, despite decades of research and growing awareness of the significance of religious actors, points to a more fundamental underlying problem – an absence of critical reflection and analysis of what "religion" means and is in contexts of development and complex humanitarian emergencies, and on the attitudes and assumptions that facilitate these simplistic and reductionist understandings of a complex multi-faceted phenomenon.

This chapter applies the critical intersectional framework developed in Chapter 2 to the study of religion, international development, and humanitarianism. It begins with a brief appraisal of recent scholarship that demonstrates the impact of secular assumptions and biases on how development is approached and carried out, drawing out the potential detrimental consequences of dominant secular paradigms. It then moves to discuss the specific context of the sector we refer to as international development and humanitarianism, emphasising that "development" is a domain that cuts across geographic boundaries and takes place in international institutions as well as in small community-based settings at the peripheries of global power. These multi-level spaces and places, with diverse and at times incompatible and contradictory language and discourses, all form part of the context in which development and humanitarianism takes place, and thus must also form part of any critical analysis of the category of religion.

Against this background, the chapter then explores the place of religious actors, identities, and narratives in relation to three core challenges on the contemporary development and humanitarianism agenda: gender equality, climate change, and migration. There are

64 *Religion in International Aid and Humanitarianism*

obviously any number of issues that could be taken as cases here. I have selected these three because (a) they form crucial components of the Sustainable Development Goals (SDGs) agenda that currently provides the overarching framework through which development programming is designed and implemented; (b) approaches to religion in relation to these three cases are often coloured by the dominant views outlined in Chapter 1 – religion as Good or Bad, Central or Marginal – contributing to one-dimensional analyses that miss important nuances.

Further, the emphasis given to these three issues and the way they are conceptualised and approached within international development and humanitarianism demonstrate the implicit power inequalities that exist within this sector. These issues are treated as more serious, more acute, more challenging in so-called "developing" areas. This framing means that the culpability of developed countries for the underlying causes of climate change and migration, for example, is an ongoing question of justice that has been insufficiently addressed. It also reinforces a paternalistic colonial relationship between developed and under-developed countries and regions of the world (Johnson 2022). Donor governments and agencies from the Global North often determine the design and implementation of projects in the Global South, yet without sufficient consideration of local context and dynamics or consultation with local communities (Luetz and Nunn 2020). It is a fact that the impacts of climate change are being felt more acutely in less developed communities. It is also a fact that the majority of displaced people (83%) are currently hosted in low- and middle-income countries (UNHCR 2022). Higher rates of gender-based violence and gender inequality are also statistically demonstrable in under-developed regions of the world (WHO 2021). These challenges are experienced differently in diverse parts of the world and it is important that we do not obfuscate those significant diversities. At the same time, while gender equality, climate change, and migration may be more acute in under-developed countries, they are by no means absent or "solved" in developed contexts. They are global problems, with local impacts, and there is much that governments, civil society, and local communities can learn from one another in how they have attempted to address them. In focusing on these challenges, the chapter makes a case for moving away from the idea of "development" to global partnership and cooperation, equalising the development playing field through mutual learning and knowledge sharing.

A word on terminology – I am here utilising "international development and humanitarianism" to refer primarily to the sector within

*Religion in International Aid and Humanitarianism*   65

global politics dealing with international economic inequality and poverty reduction; emergency humanitarian relief, including natural disasters, famine, conflict, and forced migration; the promotion of economic, social, and cultural rights; and, more recently, climate justice and the SDGs. A distinction between development and humanitarianism can be drawn with reference to time scales, in that humanitarianism often takes place in response to sudden onset emergency events, such as war and natural disasters, while development is focused on longer-term goals (Bartelink and Le Roux 2018). Yet this distinction does not always hold fast, if we consider humanitarian support provided to people in long-term displacement situations, such as Palestinian refugees living in UNRWA[1] camps in Jordan and Lebanon, for example. The cases presented are brief and preliminary. The complexity of issues and actors within gender equality, climate change, and migration fills entire books on its own. My aim here is to provide a broad brushstrokes overview and tools for approaching the topic of religion in a more comprehensive way, which can then be used as a departure point for further in-depth study and analysis.

## From Pariah to Partner: Religion in International Development and Humanitarianism

The international community has increasingly embraced the importance of attention for religion in development and humanitarianism since the 1990s (Marshall and Keough 2004). New initiatives focused on religion have sprung up around the globe. For example, the German Federal Ministry for Economic Cooperation and Development hosts and funds the International Partnership on Religion and Development (PaRD). Inter-governmental agencies, such as UNFPA and UNHCR, which have partnered with faith-based organisations since their beginning, have taken care to formalise and explicitly articulate how and why they partner with religious actors (UNFPA 2009; UNHCR 2014). UN Secretaries General Kofi Annan (2015), Ban Ki-moon (2008; 2009), and António Guterres (2019; 2021) have all stressed the importance of religious actors in realising the SDGs, tackling climate change, and addressing the global displacement crisis.

Religion has not always enjoyed such widespread support as an actor in international aid and development (and indeed strong suspicion and scepticism towards religious actors in development and humanitarianism persists). While 19th-century missionary efforts are widely acknowledged as the predecessors of modern development work (Lynch 2011; Lynch and Schwarz 2016), a pronounced pendulum swing away

## 66  *Religion in International Aid and Humanitarianism*

from religion occurred as part of the post-World War II push for modernisation. Economic and political development required modernisation, which, in turn, required, amongst other things, secularisation: the decline in the influence of "superstition" and "irrational belief" and an increase in reliance on scientific evidence, perpetuating the underlying assumption that "religion" and traditional knowledge systems are irrational and thus incompatible with "rational" science (Wilson 2012). Perhaps in part because of their association with the missionary, colonial past, religious actors became suspect within development and humanitarianism. The overarching commitment to neutrality in development and humanitarianism automatically disqualifies religious actors, the prevailing wisdom holds. Religious actors are, by definition, subjective and partial, potentially privileging the needs and interests of their own followers over those from other communities and may take advantage of people in vulnerable situations for purposes of conversion (Jones and Petersen 2011; Lynch and Schwarz 2016). These assumptions have been shaped by the underlying attitudes towards religion noted in Chapter 1 (Ngo 2018; Wilkinson 2020). Despite the increased interest in and willingness to engage with religious actors that has emerged in the 21st century, these qualms about the involvement of religious actors in development and humanitarianism persist.

This increasing engagement with religion has not been unconditional and neither has it been without its problems. There continue to be concerns amongst religious actors in development and humanitarianism about the instrumentalisation of religion (Karam 2012, 10–11). This stems from a pervasive focus on the "added value" that religious organisations bring to secular development projects, emphasised by secular and religious actors alike. The underlying narrative here assumes that development and humanitarianism are essentially secular activities. This attitude is grounded in the commitment to neutrality that is central to development and humanitarianism. Secularism is assumed to be the best way to achieve neutrality, because it is in theory agnostic about the value of religion in general and of specific religions in particular. For religious actors to have a seat at the table and be considered legitimate partners for inter-governmental agencies and secular NGOs, they must demonstrate what they contribute to development that cannot be done by secular actors. What this leads to in many instances is a strategic, perfunctory cooperation with religious actors – utilising their networks of volunteers, their ability to fundraise, and their influence in society, for example – rather than building meaningful relationships and deeply and seriously engaging with their core values and beliefs (Ager and Ager 2011; Kidwai 2016).

*Religion in International Aid and Humanitarianism* 67

Different analyses of religious actors in development and humanitarianism highlight a growing tendency to define and differentiate themselves more explicitly in either "secular" or "religious" terms. Some self-identified religious development and humanitarian agencies are increasingly secularising their organisations and activities to fit with broader standards and practices in the sector (Lynch 2011; Barnett and Stein 2012). Others are moving instead to define themselves solely as religious communities focused on worship, rituals, beliefs, and practices to avoid having to adapt their attitudes and practices to fit with growing professionalisation of the sector, a trend which some actors see as creeping secularisation (Ngo 2018).

These moves to professionalise/secularise are arguably also motivated by the growing influence of neoliberal principles and practices in the development and humanitarianism sector. Similar to what has been observed in domestic welfare provision (e.g. Williams, Cloke and Thomas 2012), states are increasingly outsourcing their aid and development responsibilities to civil society and private corporations. In this environment, NGOs and FBOs must conform to market-based performance indicators, such as "cost-effectiveness", "competitiveness", and the achievement of "deliverables", usually set by external government donors (Barnett and Stein 2012, 24). The underlying implication here is that "religious" organisations, by definition, are unprofessional, because they are not "modern" and not "secular". Some scholars (e.g. Hopgood and Vinjamuri 2012) have argued that increasing secularisation and professionalisation of the development sector is beneficial, because it guards against abuses of power by religious organisations who may take advantage of people in vulnerable situations for the purposes of conversion. What such a view fails to acknowledge, however, is that secular actors are just as capable of abuses of power and taking advantage of vulnerable people, as the sexual abuse scandal that rocked Oxfam UK in 2018 and 2021 demonstrates (BBC 2021). Secular "awareness raising activities" can be equally normative, biased, and exclusionary as religious activities (Ager and Ager 2011). Rather than being agnostic about religion, secularisms are often based on clear and strong opinions about religion's relevance and positive or negative influence, as we saw in Chapter 1. In some ways, secular activities can arguably be more problematic because they are presented as neutral, rather than encouraging open, critical reflection on the values, assumptions, and biases implicit in secular development projects.

In addition to neoliberalism, the pervasive extremism lens has also affected work in development and humanitarianism. Development practitioners note that emphasis in donor funding has shifted from a

## 68 *Religion in International Aid and Humanitarianism*

focus on poverty reduction, peacebuilding, and conflict transformation to countering violent extremism (CVE). This has contributed to crowding out other important issues, such as healthcare and education, from the agenda, unless they can somehow be justified as forms of CVE (Harper 2019, 221–222). In some respects, this emphasis fits with other prevailing assumptions governing development assistance and humanitarianism – for example, that a reduction in violence and insecurity will contribute to the general flourishing of the population and the protection and upholding of human rights (Chowdhury Fink and Bhulai 2016). Yet CVE policies and initiatives can result in the exaggerated targeting of specific countries and populations, identified based on their (assumed) religious identity. This targeting has had particularly damaging consequences in migration, where "refugee", "Muslim", and "terrorist" have become inextricably entangled in public discourse and contributed to further securitisation of migration and antagonism towards people fleeing violence and persecution (Wilson and Mavelli 2016). There has been an observable increase in focus on religious identity of both recipients and providers of development and humanitarian assistance in the 21st century. In the post-9/11 environment, for example, migrants have increasingly been described with reference to their religious identity, where prior to 9/11 their ethnic identity had been emphasised (Mudde 2019). The publication of UNHCR and UNFPA partnership notes for working with faith-based actors – despite having already been working with faith-based actors for decades without such explicit guidelines – highlights the increasing sensitivity to "religion" in general. Delineating how and when such organisations work with "religious actors" as well as clearer distinctions between who is and who is not a "legitimate" religious actor to partner with also speaks to the growing preoccupation with distinguishing between "good" and "bad" religion (Fiddian-Qasmiyeh 2014; 2016).

Underpinning these prevailing approaches, we can see the influence of the "Two Faces of Faith" approach. Religion is presented as both the source of pressing issues and concerns in development and humanitarianism and the panacea to solve these urgent challenges (Fiddian-Qasmiyeh 2014; 2016; Hurd 2015). As we have seen throughout this book, placing too much focus on "religion" as an explanatory factor in world politics can be just as damaging as placing too little focus on it. This is particularly the case when we do not take the time and care to define and understand precisely what is meant by "religion" across the multiple and infinitely varied contexts in which international development and humanitarianism take place.

## The Context of International Development and Humanitarianism

Defining and delving into the context of international development and humanitarianism is complicated, because it takes place in situations where layer upon layer of political and cultural meanings, discourses, and practices are intermingled. Consequently, considering the space and place as well as the language and discourses present is crucial for appreciating the full spectrum of nuances and complexities affecting how development and humanitarianism projects and interventions are designed and carried out. The project my colleague and I were asked to evaluate provides a concrete example. Part of this research included visiting a community in Nakuru, Kenya, where the national office of the FBO we were working with was implementing a project promoting gender equality. There was a local office in Nakuru, as well as staff from the national office in Nairobi. Yet the project was funded by an office of the same organisation based in Melbourne, Australia, and overseen by yet another office situated in the Netherlands. Overlaying all these different actors and cultures are the broad international structures and coalitions of actors, agreed principles of neutrality and impartiality in the delivery of aid, and the global framework of the SDGs. In one day, my colleague and I went from conversations with women in Nakuru concerning the distribution of household chores, instances of gender-based violence in the community and the social and cultural taboos that continued to inhibit reporting and prosecution of rape, to discussions about the 1995 Beijing Platform for Action, the SDGs, theologies of gender equality, the expectations of the Australian donors regarding the programme outcomes and what the evaluation report should address, as well as the reflections of the Dutch directors of the global programme. Add to these layers differences in how specific terms are used and understood across each of these different levels of interest and influence in development and humanitarianism – for example, "Beijing" was widely used and understood as referring to the Platform for Action by interlocutors in Nairobi, but unheard of in Nakuru, while "gender equality" was replaced with "relations between men and women". All these different threads, set against the backdrop of the broader contours of international development and humanitarianism, such as increasing neoliberalisation and emphasis on extremism discussed above, create the context in which international development and humanitarian projects and interventions take place (see Figure 4.1).

When analysing "religion" in international development and humanitarianism, we must bear all of these interwoven elements in mind – the specific geographic, cultural, historical, and political context where the project is taking place; the diverse national political and cultural characters each of the different stakeholders (donors, implementers, support offices) bring to the project, even when those different offices or stakeholders all ostensibly represent the same organisation, just from different parts of the world; the transnational development sector, international institutions, and overarching frameworks that provide the broad contours and justifications for funding such development projects; the history of the development sector and its problematic relationship with (neo-)colonial and missionary agendas; and the challenge of diverse languages and discourses, where terms do not necessarily mean the same thing from one register to the next (see also Grüll and Wilson 2018).

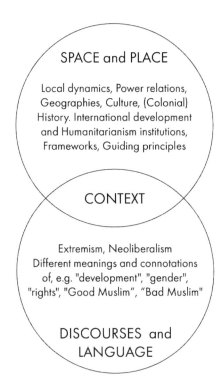

*Figure 4.1* The Context of Religion, Development, and Humanitarianism.
Image Credit: Jessica Mills Designs.

## Religious Actors, Identities, and Narratives in Development and Humanitarianism

Simply discussing "religion" in international development and humanitarianism does not do justice to the almost dizzying array of actors, identities, and narratives at play in this sector. Gerard Clarke (2006) identifies five main types of faith-based actors represented in international development (though there are an infinite number of variations on each of these types). These range from representative apex bodies, charitable NGOs, socio-political organisations, missionary organisations, and, in Clarke's analysis, terrorist organisations. The language within the sector has shifted in recent years to incorporate not just "faith-based organisations" but also "local faith communities" and "faith leaders" (e.g. UNHCR 2014). The preponderance of the word "faith" is often critiqued for suggesting an implicitly Euro-American centric understanding of "religion", with an emphasis on religious belief, participation, and identification as issues of personal choice and commitment. Emphasis on "faith" immediately limits understanding of what "religion" is across the diverse contexts where international development and humanitarianism take place. This has prompted a move away from "faith" towards "religion" or "religions" (Tomalin 2021) to create space for diverse actors and influences to be included under this umbrella.

Utilising the categories developed in Chapter 2 provides the possibility for being even more precise when it comes to the different ways that "religion" matters in international development and humanitarianism (see Figure 4.2). Within research there is a prevailing focus on the different types of religious actors that are present within international development and humanitarianism, while less attention is paid to identities and narratives. Arguably, this is reflective of criticism raised by religious actors in the development sector themselves – the charge of instrumentalisation. While there has been increasing interest in cooperating with religious actors amongst secular agencies and international organisations, this often occurs in strategic ways that do not engage deeply, meaningfully, and seriously with the beliefs and values of religious actors (Kidwai 2016). This manner of engagement, they opine, is superficial and does not contribute to building long-term partnerships based on equality and mutual respect. Secular actors and the secular framework governing development remain dominant. It is important to emphasise that religious actors are just as capable of instrumentalising cooperation with secular agencies in the pursuit of their own goals and agendas. Nonetheless, a failure to understand and

72  *Religion in International Aid and Humanitarianism*

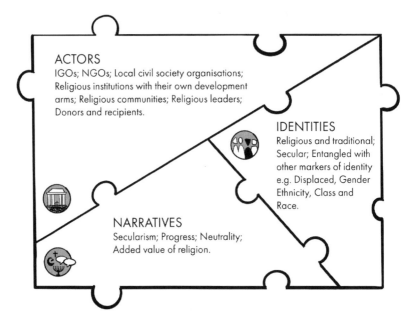

*Figure 4.2* Religious Actors, Identities, and Narratives in Development and Humanitarianism.
Image Credit: Jessica Mills Designs.

engage with the identities, values, and narratives that drive the activities of religious actors or that influence specific development contexts and humanitarian emergencies can lead to failures of development projects and emergency humanitarian relief efforts. We will explore these effects further in discussions of specific issues below.

## Gender Equality

Projects promoting gender equality within the development sector have been especially impacted by assumptions about "religion". There has been and continues to be an underlying presumption that religious actors are inherently antagonistic towards gender equality, that religious narratives reinforce patriarchal norms and social structures, and that if individuals and communities identify themselves (or are identified by others) by their religious affiliation, this automatically precludes action on gender equality, or at the very least improving the situation of women and LGBTQI+ people will be slow and face

*Religion in International Aid and Humanitarianism*   73

multiple obstacles. A strong binary opposition between religion and gender equality is present within development and humanitarianism, shaped by secular feminist attitudes: religion and gender equality cannot co-exist. Religious actors and institutions will oppose gender equality. These implicit assumptions are premised on the understanding of religion as traditional, oppressive, and homogenous (Daulatzai 2004).

It cannot be denied that religious actors, identities, and narratives have often either opposed gender equality or been deployed in opposition to efforts to promote the rights of women and LGBTQI+ people. Yet to approach all religious actors with the prior assumption that they uphold patriarchal values and gender inequality is both limiting and misleading. It is limiting in the sense that religious actors are often highly influential in their communities and consequently are often key to transforming social attitudes around gender identities and gender roles (Bartelink 2021). It is misleading in that it overlooks the important work being done by many self-identified religious actors to challenge and overturn patriarchal structures, traditional gender norms, and damaging attitudes towards sexuality and gender-based violence that are particularly harmful for women and LGBTQI+ people. It also precludes critique of secular agencies, organisations, and contexts that also struggle with gender inequality (Scott 2018). The problem is not religion, and nor is it secularism. Sexism, misogyny, and patriarchy are the problems in and of themselves. These problems and attitudes exist in all contexts, though they are arguably more subtle and insidious in some contexts than in others. They are often entangled with other social and political factors and ways of thinking, including religion, but they cut across the artificial distinction of "religion" and "secular" (Scott 2018). Below, I include a brief discussion of the work of religious actors in development that provides an example of efforts to disrupt and challenge these assumed links between religion and conservative, traditional, patriarchal gender attitudes, one an international FBO, the other a national organisation working with diverse local communities in Indonesia.

### *World Vision International's Channels of Hope Programme*

The international Protestant Christian NGO World Vision (WV) has been running its Channels of Hope Gender (CoHG) programme for almost two decades. Channels of Hope (CoH) itself first began as a programme to challenge ignorance and stigmatisation of people living with HIV and has subsequently been adapted to versions that engage

## 74 *Religion in International Aid and Humanitarianism*

attitudes of suspicion, reluctance, opposition, or ignorance around gender equality; maternal, newborn, and child health; child protection; Ebola (World Vision International 2016); and most recently the COVID-19 vaccination (Mofya 2022). While developed by a self-identified Protestant Christian NGO, the model has been effectively adapted and deployed in ecumenical contexts involving Catholic and Orthodox communities, as well as in multi-faith communities involving people identifying as both Christian and Muslim, often entangled with local indigenous belief systems. In undertaking this deployment in multi-faith contexts, WV has worked with other religious NGOs, such as Islamic Relief, religious scholars from diverse faith traditions, and in collaboration with local religious and traditional leaders (Bartelink and Wilson 2020). CoH thus offers a malleable and adaptable model that considers the specificities of local contexts. It brings scientifically grounded research and evidence in conversation with religious norms, texts, and principles to address social and community values that may be harmful to overall individual and community health and well-being. Staff from World Vision International (WVI) work with staff and leadership in national and local WV field offices to introduce the programme into local communities in collaboration with local religious and community leaders. These local leaders then establish training and action teams with members from local communities (Congregational or Community Hope Action Teams (CHATs)) who meet on a regular basis to plan and implement activities to address issues and challenges related to the specific area of focus. What we can see already is that, just within the CoH example itself, there are multiple different kinds of religious actors involved – a large international FBO, local and national offices of that FBO, local religious communities, and individual religious leaders, many of whom defy traditional stereotypes and expectations of who exactly "religious leaders" are.

The foundational assumptions driving the CoH programme are based on a recognition that introducing laws to promote gender equality or child protection is not always enough to prevent and eradicate harmful assumptions and practices. Core attitudes and behaviours must also be addressed. In multiple contexts, these underlying attitudes and assumptions are influenced by prevailing religious and cultural norms and narratives. Such assumptions include notions of the man as the head of the household, with power and authority over his wife, and distinct, separate gender roles, resulting in women carrying out a disproportionate amount of domestic labour. WVI states that the goal of the programme is not to change local beliefs but rather to explore how these beliefs could be compatible with attitudes that support equal rights of men and women, and reinterpreted to reduce instances of gender-based violence, for instance, shifting away from seeing the man as the head of the household to a view of spouses as equal partners who support each other (WVI 2016). The extent to which such an intervention can be considered as simply "reinterpreting" religious texts, beliefs, and norms or actually "changing" them is debatable.

The programme has provided constructive support for efforts to address and reduce harmful attitudes and practices towards gender equality and gender-based violence, as a colleague and I discovered during fieldwork carried out between 2014 and 2017 (Bartelink and Wilson 2020 see Figure 4.3). Interviewees from communities in Malawi, Kenya, South Africa, and Tanzania stated that after participating in the CoHG programmes, spouses were more focused on harmonious relations and mutual support than adhering to traditional gender roles. This shift in attitudes resulted in concrete changes, with men taking on more domestic chores, supporting their wives before, during, and after childbirth, and reduced instances of domestic violence. It is important to note that these changes were reported anecdotally, not statistically. Statistical data is largely non-existent in many of the contexts where we conducted research. It is also possible that some of our interlocutors were telling us what they thought we wanted to hear, as white Western researchers being brought in by the organisation running the programme. Yet, the responses of our interlocutors were not just positive. They also voiced criticisms of the programme and offered suggestions for its improvement.

*Figure 4.3* Focus Group discussions with CoHG participants in Nakuru, Kenya.
Source: B.E. Bartelink.

## 76 *Religion in International Aid and Humanitarianism*

CoHG and programmes like it are not silver bullets that solve all challenges surrounding the intersection of religion, gender, and development. The emphasis of the programme is on relations between men and women, with no attention for the rights and equality of LGBTQI+ people, which remains taboo in many contexts. Further, a recurrent issue we observed was that implicitly "leadership" was assumed by participants and WV staff alike to be a male role (Bartelink and Wilson 2020, 53). At the same time, CoHG empowered women and created space for them to develop as leaders in different ways, shaping and influencing their communities beyond the avenues open to those (usually men) occupying traditional institutional religious leadership roles. This last point is an important insight for broader work on religion, development, and humanitarianism. "Leadership" comes in many styles and forms. Governments, NGOs, and other development and humanitarianism actors must go beyond the usual suspects and think outside of stereotypical institutional religious leadership roles when partnering with religious actors for social transformation.

Within CoHG, we see the significance of expanding the way we analyse the category of religion. The actors involved in CoHG are diverse and multi-faceted and may not always align with established ideas of who exactly "religious" actors are. Within the communities where it is implemented, CoHG works to challenge pervasive religious and cultural narratives about gender identities and roles. Concurrently, communication about CoHG with external actors, such as governments and other NGOs, seeks to disrupt dominant secular narratives circulating in development about religion's irrelevance to or harmful impact on the promotion of gender equality. It is important to remember, though, that these insights should not be generalised. They are informed by the diverse contexts in which CoHG takes place. The significance and characteristics of religious actors, identities, and narratives shifts with each different project, case, or context, as we will observe with the discussion of Fahmina and Mosintuwu in Indonesia.

### Fahmina and Mosintuwu, Indonesia

Whilst often referred to as the largest Muslim-majority democracy in the world, Indonesia is perhaps better understood as super-diverse (Becci, Burchardt and Giorda 2016) when it comes to the multifarious religious and belief communities, traditions, and identities present within Indonesian society. Amongst the Muslim-majority population there are Sunni, Shia, and Ahmadiyya communities, and significant intrareligious diversity exists within these groups. Multiple other

*Religion in International Aid and Humanitarianism* 77

religious and belief communities are also part of the fabric of Indonesian society, including diverse Christian, Buddhist, Hindu, Confucian, and tribal traditions (Laksana and Wood 2019), as well as a somewhat clandestine but nonetheless vibrant atheist community (Duile 2018).

Being conscious of this diversity is essential when examining women's rights and gender equality in Indonesia. A strong tendency exists within development, feminist, and human rights literature, policymaking, and advocacy to assume that overtly religious (especially Muslim) societies are characterised by conservative attitudes towards women's rights and gender equality (Daulatzai 2004). It must be acknowledged that there are dominant voices within Indonesian politics and society that promote traditional gender roles for women and seek to restrict their rights and freedoms, often using religious justifications (Wieringa 2015). These narratives are perhaps more aptly described as "religio-political", however, since these positions include an argument that notions of gender equality and women's rights are imposed by Western powers and Western-dominated institutions (Dzuhayatin 2015, 30; Wieringa 2015, 36). Opposition to women's rights and gender equality could be read as anti-colonial and anti-Western as much as it is "religious". While these voices may be the most prominent or may be given the most attention within mainstream global politics and media, perspectives on women's rights and gender equality in Indonesia are anything but homogenous.

Two grassroots community organisations in Indonesia provide examples. Fahmina, based in Cirebon, and Mosintuwu, based in Sulawesi, both engage in a plethora of projects and activities related to human rights, intra- and inter-religious dialogue and engagement, promotion of the right to freedom of religion or belief, addressing hate speech, and advocating for gender equality and the rights of women. Both organisations are long-term partners of Dutch faith-based development organisation, Mensen met een Missie (MM). It is in the context of this partnership and my own ongoing research collaboration with MM that I encountered Fahmina and Mosintuwu.[2] The material discussed below was collected through interviews and participant observation during two periods of fieldwork carried out by our Groningen-based research team, as well as online consultations with staff from both organisations.

Fahmina focuses explicitly on promoting and strengthening the role and position of women in society through engagement with religious arguments, texts, rituals, and practices. They have established a network with women *ulama* (scholars) across Indonesia to support them in their work in Muslim communities. Fahmina have also developed

## 78 *Religion in International Aid and Humanitarianism*

a national media campaign and strategy that directly challenges conservative Muslim and anti-Western narratives regarding women's rights and gender equality. Fahmina highlight that conservative Muslim attitudes towards women's rights and gender equality are often shaped by actors external to Indonesia. To counter this influence, the organisation draws on indigenous Indonesian Islamic scholarship that offers alternative interpretations of Islamic texts and traditions that are consistent with a broader human rights agenda and support greater gender equality, encourages more awareness of and opposition to domestic and gender-based violence, and promotes women's rights. Yet, like many actors in international development and humanitarianism, Fahmina are well-versed in speaking different languages to different publics. In their advocacy and campaigning targeting national level politicians and institutions they refer to Islamic discourses and international human rights norms. Yet when they work with local communities in Cirebon, they often avoid direct reference to religion or human rights, instead translating or vernacularising norms and values from international human rights into concepts and terms that make sense in the everyday language and context of Cirebon (Grüll and Wilson 2018; Wilson 2022b).

Mosintuwu, based in Sulawesi and established and led by award-winning human rights activist Lian Gogali (see Figure 4.4), is an organisation run by women, for women. Mosintuwu and Gogali provide an example of the importance of going beyond stereotypical assumptions regarding who "religious actors" and "religious leaders" are when it comes to analysing religion in development and humanitarianism. Dominant assumptions about religious actors are often highly gendered, assuming that religious organisations, leaders, and institutions are predominantly masculine. Mosintuwu directly counters that overarching assumption. Further, where dominant narratives of development and human rights often place women's rights and religion in opposition to one another, Mosintuwu deliberately brings them together, focusing on building relationships amongst women across diverse religious communities through education and emancipation. In this way, the organisation is focused on reducing inter-religious conflict in the Poso region of Sulawesi through the empowerment and healing of women (Kristimanta 2021). In part, this strategy is shaped by the pervasiveness of religious identities in Poso, as well as the recognition that conflict impacts women in unique ways that can be acutely harmful to the achievement of their rights. Again, however, Mosintuwu do not always utilise the language of human rights, nor do they explicitly refer to or discuss different religious identities and communities, since direct reference to these topics can provoke suspicion and opposition, or simply do not connect with the lived realities of women participating in the activities organised by Mosintuwu.

Understanding the social and political landscape regarding religion and gender equality in Indonesia highlights how important it is to move beyond the established assumptions and stereotypes associated with the category of religion as well as specific religions. While it is a Muslim-majority democracy, Indonesia is also incredibly intra- and inter-religiously diverse. This rich religious landscape is of vital importance for appreciating the multifarious perspectives that exist regarding the connection between religion and gender equality, that there is no singular, homogenous position when it comes to the attitudes of religious actors towards women's rights. It reminds us again that context is crucial; that the category of religion means different things in different places; that religious actors are widely divergent. Religious actors may even oppose one another's positions on issues such as gender diversity, whilst claiming legitimacy and authority from the same sacred texts, rituals, and traditions, as is the case with conservative Muslim political elites in Indonesia on the one hand and organisations

*Figure 4.4* Mosintuwu Founder and Director, Lian Gogali, (seated with computer) and her team in Poso, Indonesia.
Source: Mensen met een Missie.

## 80  *Religion in International Aid and Humanitarianism*

like Fahmina and Mosintuwu on the other. This diversity of attitudes towards socio-political issues within and amongst diverse religious traditions is also a defining feature when we consider the intersection of "religion" with climate change in contexts of development, as we shall see further below.

### Climate Change

The impacts of climate change are being increasingly felt across all development and humanitarian work. Its nature as an all-encompassing global challenge means that not only is climate change an area of focus in its own right, but it is also an aspect of consideration for all other issues, from poverty reduction to conflict and peacebuilding (Tarusarira 2022), to human rights (Bell 2013) and gender equality (Lau et al. 2021). It is well-documented that the most severe impacts of climate change will be and indeed already have been felt by the poorest and most vulnerable communities globally (Tanner and Horn-Phathanothai 2014).

The category of religion is entangled with climate change and development in diverse and complex ways. Dominant traditional discourses regarding religion and climate change that stem from a priori assumptions about what religion is and focus on its level and type of influence tend only to focus either on the destructive influence of religion and its contribution to logic that facilitates harmful environmental attitudes or practices, or on its constructive contribution to shifting mindsets and urging responsibility for the planet. The work of Lynn White (1967) epitomises the former. White argued that Christianity, with its Genesis 1:28 command to "fill the earth and subdue it" (ironically a verse from the Hebrew Bible, and so not only part of the Christian tradition), contributed to the creation of a binary between humanity and nature. Humanity and the natural environment were separated as part of this dualistic logic. Humanity was positioned as superior and nature as subservient to the needs of humanity, opening the way for human exploitation of nature.[3] White's analysis has been highly influential when it comes to approaches towards religion and climate change, contributing to permeating assumptions that religion, especially Christianity, is at best irrelevant and at worst culpable when it comes to climate change and environmental destruction. Hence, action on climate change has, until recently, tended to ignore or sideline contributions from religious actors and narratives (Hulme 2017). Yet it has also contributed to assumptions about non-Christian, non-Western philosophies, and

*Religion in International Aid and Humanitarianism* 81

traditions, such as Buddhism and Shintoism, as more environmentally conscious, assumptions that do not always reflect realities on the ground and again contribute to homogenising and simplifying diverse communities and experiences (Swearer 2006; Rots 2015).

Pope Francis' 2015 *Laudato Si* did much to address this widely held view of religion's destructive contribution towards climate change. It is often upheld as an example of the second perspective, emphasising the God-given role and responsibility that humanity has to protect and care for nature, to be good stewards, ensuring the continuation of species and a healthy planet for future generations. This perspective is often premised on the exact same verse as the more destructive approaches critiqued by White yet interpreted differently. It is important here to highlight the political diversity of attitudes within and amongst religious actors. For example, the Catholic Church under Pope Francis has adopted stances on issues such as climate change and migration that could be characterised as politically progressive (Deneulin 2021), while its position on gender equality, women's rights, and the rights of LGBTQI+ people are often described as politically conservative (Bartelink 2021). This in turn results in diverse coalitions of religious actors advocating on particular issues. The actors with whom the Catholic Church partners on advocacy for climate change may well be their opponents in debates on gender equality and the rights of LGBTQI+ people (Bartelink 2021). Understanding "religion" and religious actors in homogenised ways as only conservative and traditional or only progressive and modern fails to do justice to the intricacy and complexity of the perspectives and allegiances at play.

These reductionist approaches to "religion" have contributed to the failure of climate change adaptation and mitigation policies in several contexts. A growing body of literature has identified religion as a "barrier" to or justification for lack of action on climate change in Small Island Developing States (SIDS) (Mortreux and Barnett 2009; Klöck 2015). In these analyses, we can see the influence of dominant secular narratives governing the development and humanitarian sector – religion is irrational, pre-modern, and a hindrance to "progress", while development is rational and modern, a conduit for "advancing" society. On the specific issue of climate change, this assumption is exacerbated by the construction of climate change as a predominantly "scientific" issue, thereby excluding any consideration of religion's relationship with climate change because of its assumed "irrational" nature. This construction, however, is highly limiting, restricting thinking on climate change to scientific and technical domains and solutions, and positioning "religion" in opposition to "science". Yet the implications of climate change

82  *Religion in International Aid and Humanitarianism*

extend well beyond these realms to the domains of politics, economics, culture, morality, and spirituality, by raising existential anxieties about the survival of the human species and the planet (Wilson 2022a).

Patrick Nunn (2017) flips the dominant discourse about religion and climate change by questioning the secular development approach itself. Rather than religion being to blame for the failure of SIDS to act on climate change or the ineffectiveness of foreign aid projects on climate change adaptation and mitigation, Nunn (2017) and Luetz and Nunn (2020) suggest that the failure of climate adaptation and mitigation development projects in SIDS, specifically the Pacific Islands, is instead a failure of development agencies and donors to engage with and take seriously the worldviews of people and communities in the areas where projects are being implemented. The solution is not simply that we need to pay more attention to "religion". There needs to be a shift in emphasis from centralising secular modern development discourses to instead privileging the perspectives of the communities in which development projects are being undertaken, including those where "religion" in all its diverse manifestations is dominant. Luetz and Nunn (2020) posit that it may in fact be the secularism of international development that is the obstacle, because it does not address the existing societal realities and prevailing modes of understanding in target communities. This paradigm shift is imperative for effective action on climate change and development and humanitarian projects more broadly. Luetz and Nunn's (2020) argument resonates with the broader argument of this book, the importance of context and of understanding the actors, identities, and narratives that are most significant in specific contexts, rather than generalising from the subjective positionality of the Euro-American experience.

### Climate Adaptation in the Pacific

SIDS in the Pacific will be, and are already, some of the communities most adversely affected by climate change. Governments within the Pacific and donor agencies supporting development projects in the region have been promoting the need for climate change adaptation measures for several decades now (Bertana 2021). Yet they frequently lament the slowness or in some cases absolute failure of some communities, particularly those in remote parts of the islands, to implement adequate adaptation measures, such as relocating to higher ground in light of increased flooding events, freshwater salinisation, and the expected continued rise of sea levels. While not the only factor identified as contributing to resistance to adaptation measures, several studies

*Religion in International Aid and Humanitarianism* 83

have highlighted religion as a barrier to climate change adaptation (Lata and Nunn 2012; Piggott-McKellar et al. 2019; Bertana 2021). Describing religion as a "barrier" or "obstacle" to climate change adaptation already highlights some of the problematic underlying assumptions about both "religion" and the communities of SIDS that affect climate adaptation efforts. It suggests, first, an undifferentiated approach to understanding what religion is and how it manifests in the Pacific. Second, it privileges the view of Western, secular, development practitioners, rather than the communities themselves. As Piggott-McKellar et al. (2019, 384) highlight, "barriers can be defined differently by different actors". For the communities themselves, religion is not an optional extra or an add-on to their lives but is interwoven into the fabric of their individual and collective existence. It is an inextricable part of their existential reality – it is how their world works (Blaser 2013) – not something that they choose to adhere to or not. It suggests a failure on the part of foreign aid policymakers and development practitioners to adequately appreciate all dimensions of the contexts in which they work, in particular religion.

### *Religious Actors, Identities, Discourses*

While there is a diversity of religious traditions and communities present across the Pacific region, including Hinduism, Islam, and Buddhism, Christianity is by far the dominant faith tradition, often intermingled with traditional indigenous spirituality (Nunn et al. 2016; Bertana 2021). As with gender equality, diverse kinds of religious actors across multiple levels are active in the Pacific region working on climate change. One of the largest organisations is the Pacific Conference of Churches (PCC), headquartered in Suva, Fiji. A consortium of churches from across a variety of denominations, the PCC boasts member churches from 19 countries across the region (PCC 2022). The PCC has been a leading body in raising awareness about the impacts of climate change in the region and the necessity for urgent adaptation measures. Working closely with government and other non-government agencies, the PCC collaborates on climate adaptation measures, providing support through research, advice, and networking (Bertana 2021). The PCC was also responsible for the drafting and publication of the "first" Moana Declaration[4] in 2009, accepting the science of climate change, acknowledging the impacts it was already having in communities, and issuing a call to action for churches and their congregations (WCC 2009).

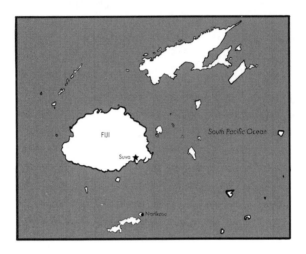

*Figure 4.5* Map of Fiji.
Image Credit: Jessica Mills Designs.

The PCC's messages and discourse on climate change and the representative bodies of its member churches do not always resonate with local congregations, particularly in more remote parts of the Pacific. This reinforces the observation that religions are not homogenous. When it comes to development programming and project implementation, it is crucial that scholars and practitioners go beyond these leadership bodies and engage with the populations in the community congregations. At the local level, there is a high degree of scepticism towards scientific knowledge. While in part this is because belief and faith in God trumps trust in science, it is also partially because of the way scientific messages on climate change have been communicated in these areas. As Bertana (2021) shares based on her fieldwork in Narikoso, Fiji (see Figure 4.5), government and secular NGO representatives frequently visit Narikoso to give workshops and seminars to raise awareness about climate change. Next to the communication of the scientific evidence, a key message of these information sessions is that villagers themselves are not responsible for climate change. They cannot do anything to stop or reverse it. They are victims of the high-consumption lifestyles and practices of people in the Global North. What they need to do is adapt to the changes that climate change is bringing, such as moving to higher ground in preparation for sea level rise. Yet this message provokes sceptical, even angry, and resentful

*Religion in International Aid and Humanitarianism* 85

responses from the local population. Bertana (2021, 86) quotes a Narikoso man in his forties: "We have been living like this for years. You come here with your science and bring fear". This response echoes observations from research on scientific communication about climate change in other contexts (O'Neill and Nicholson-Cole 2009; Norgaard 2011; Wilson 2022a). Emphasising threat and fear are not necessarily the most effective ways to encourage proactive responses regarding climate change adaptation. In Narikoso, this message did not resonate with local understandings of the world (Bertana 2021). The message that villagers had no control over climate change indirectly contributed to reinforcing the idea that God is in control, human beings are not. Local preachers highlight the story of Noah and God's promise not to flood the earth again as evidence that the islands are safe from rising sea levels and so they do not need to relocate to higher ground.

This mismatch in messaging in Narikoso is a microcosm of two interrelated problems that affect the development and humanitarian sector. On the one hand, it provides a clear example of the dominance of secular narratives and worldviews in international development, a form of injustice (Wilson 2017) that crowds out alternative "ways of worlding" (Blaser 2013), including religious, spiritual, traditional, and indigenous worldviews, from mainstream development discourses, policy planning, and implementation. This is problematic because, as we can see from the Narikoso example, the dominance of secular, scientific frameworks can in some cases hinder rather than facilitate progress on development goals.

This problem is entangled with the second, namely, that most development projects are funded by governments and agencies external to the communities and regions where they are being implemented. Consequently, they are driven by donor priorities, rather than by priorities identified by the communities themselves (Nunn et al. 2016). Some scholars have proposed that governments in developing countries "commit significant amounts of internally-generated revenue to climate-change adaptation" (Nunn et al. 2016, 491) to address the problem and gain autonomy over how climate change is communicated and how adaptation programmes are designed and implemented. While clearly and definitively addressing the problem of ownership and privileging local perspectives and narratives, this suggestion does not account for the underlying inequalities and injustices that have generated climate change, as well as broader economic and socio-political power imbalances amongst countries at the global level. Most developing countries did not contribute to the problem of climate change and have far fewer financial resources at their disposal than developed

86    *Religion in International Aid and Humanitarianism*

countries. Such suggestions for internally funded climate adaptation measures implicitly perpetuate a nation-state-centred approach to climate change (and other development challenges). Yet all countries around the globe are faced with increasingly harmful consequences from climate change. All countries grapple with the problem of gender inequality and gender-based violence. Yet so often, the issues on the development agenda are treated as though they are only problems for developing countries.

Such attitudes, whether implicit or explicit, contribute to reinforcing colonial-era power imbalances and inequalities on which the development sector was arguably founded and on which it relies for its justification and legitimacy. It suggests that the whole concept and practice of "development" needs to be rethought and replaced with a more equalised and balanced approach of partnership and mutual learning, recognising that "development" problems are experienced by all communities everywhere. They are experienced in different ways and to different extremes because of the specificities of context. Yet there is still much to be gained from approaches that privilege shared knowledge, mutual learning, and partnership, in contrast with those that reinforce traditional development paradigms built on the unequal relations between core and periphery, Global North and Global South (McMichael and Weber 2021).

## Forced Migration

The category of religion has become seemingly more significant in the context of complex humanitarian emergencies resulting from conflict, famine, climate change, and the complicated entanglement of these and other factors that force people to flee their homes. Each forced migration event has its own unique characteristics. The flight of Syrian people brought on by the decade-long Syrian civil war differs in important ways from the mass movement of people generated by the 2022 Russian invasion of Ukraine. These events and their impact on the people affected are again different from the experiences of people in situations of long-term or permanent displacement, such as Palestinians living in refugee camps in Jordan for over half a century (see Figure 4.6). Religion is entangled with each of these complex humanitarian situations, yet in highly diverse and often incomparable ways, as we shall explore further below.

Assumptions about the religious identity of displaced people can have significant consequences for both their immediate and long-term resettlement outcomes. The so-called "refugee crisis" in Europe in

*Religion in International Aid and Humanitarianism* 87

2015 offers a case in point. The vast majority of people seeking protection during this period originated from countries in the Middle East, where Islam is the majority, though by no means the only, religion. As a result of this association, people fleeing conflict in Syria, Afghanistan, Somalia, and South Sudan, amongst others, were often assumed to be Muslim. This assumption disregarded the religious diversity that exists within these countries, including the diversities within Islam itself and all the various ways there are in which to be Muslim. It further paid little, if any, attention to individual self-ascribed religious affiliations. In Canada, this materially affected where refugees were resettled, since towns that did not have a mosque were automatically excluded as resettlement options (Beaman et al. 2016). This privileging of the religious identity of people seeking asylum neglects other factors that may be of more immediate concern, such as finding employment, adequate shelter, and educational opportunities for their children. Amidst the broader context of discourses about extremism and "Good" and "Bad" Muslims (Mamdani 2002), these assumptions about the religious identity of people seeking protection contributed to them being viewed with suspicion, as potential terrorists (Wilson and Mavelli 2016), a sentiment fuelled by far-right extremist groups (as we saw in Chapter 3) and unfounded claims that Syrian refugees were involved in the terrorist attacks in Paris in 2015 (Abrams 2015; Amanpour and Patterson 2015). These views are not solely based on suspicion of Islam, however. There is also a racialised and Orientalist dimension associated with people from the Middle East seeking asylum. Chapter 2 already highlighted the divergent responses to people fleeing the Taliban in Afghanistan in August 2021 following the US withdrawal compared to emergency policies rolled out in Europe, the UK, the US, and Australia to provide protection for people fleeing the 2022 war in Ukraine. These starkly different responses are not only about religious identities. They are driven by a complex mix of assumptions regarding racial, cultural, historical, colonial, and civilisational relationships and connections. Yet religious identity is an inseparable component of those underlying assumptions.

A second area that is receiving increasing attention in the context of forced migration is the relationship between religion, spirituality, and mental health. This interest builds on recognition within psychology regarding the relationship between religious beliefs and identities and mental health. The same tendency to focus on "good" vs "bad" effects of religion on mental health is evident here, with research often emphasising the positive role that prayer and religious activity can have on peoples' mental health, alongside the detrimental toll that harmful

88    *Religion in International Aid and Humanitarianism*

or abusive religious and spiritual practices have on people (Gozdziak 2002; Koslander, da Silva and Roxberg 2009; Abdul-Hamid and Hacker Hughes 2015). Recent efforts within research on Mental Health and Psychosocial Support (MHPSS) and forced migration have attempted to complicate this good/bad narrative (Matthies-Boon 2017; Ager et al. 2019). Rather than focusing on normative judgements regarding whether religion has positive or negative impacts on the mental health of displaced people, this research instead takes for granted that religious, or more accurately existential, identities and beliefs are important for the mental health and well-being of people experiencing displacement, building on insights from spiritual care research and practice (de Haan 2017). The distinction between "religious" and "existential" matters here, since beliefs regarding the nature of reality, whether there is a transcendent reality beyond the immanent natural world, whether there is meaning and purpose to one's existence, are questions that matter for people regardless of whether they hold a religious commitment or not (de Haan 2017). The experience of forced displacement can severely disrupt individual and community beliefs on these questions, contributing to a kind of "spiritual" or "existential" trauma, on top of the physical and psychological trauma resulting from conflict and flight (Matthies-Boon 2017). Researchers working on this topic are encouraging a shift away from focusing on whether religion and spirituality are positive or negative factors in relation to the mental health of displaced people and should therefore be encouraged or avoided. The focus should be on understanding how religion, spirituality, and existential reality matters for people on the move and how the experience of displacement is affecting their spiritual well-being, distinct from their mental health (Ager, Abebe and Ager 2014).

There remains significant hesitation amongst civil society organisations and practitioners supporting people on the move around engaging explicitly with religion in MHPSS activities and programmes. In July 2017, a colleague and I conducted semi-structured interviews with 20 representatives from 12 civil society organisations working in Amman, Jordan, regarding religion, spirituality, and mental health amongst Syrian and Palestinian refugees supported by these different organisations.[5] The goal of these interviews was to, first, explore how practitioners understood the relationship between religion, spirituality, and mental health. Second, we sought to discover whether, based on practitioners' experiences and observations, religion was significant for mental health and then how it mattered. Finally, we were interested in identifying how practitioners incorporated attention for religion and spirituality into their MHPSS programming.

*Figure 4.6* Camp Al-Hussein, Palestinian refugee camp, Amman, Jordan.
Source: Hasanisawi, Wikimedia/public domain.

The organisations ranged from explicitly religious, such as World Vision Jordan, Lutheran World Foundation, and Islamic Relief, to implicitly religious (e.g. Catholic Mission Service, who are known in Amman simply as CMS and do not refer to their Catholic identity), small local Muslim organisations to international secular organisations such as the Agency for Technical Cooperation and Development (ACTED) and War Child.

All the organisations interviewed expressed an awareness of religion as an issue that is related to the effective treatment of trauma and mental health issues amongst people who are displaced. Yet this awareness comes in a variety of forms. Some of our interlocutors viewed religion as a complete "no go" topic, while others saw religion as important but were unsure how to approach it in their programmes, emphasising a need for additional resources and training. Still others incorporate religion through "shared values" – not referring to it explicitly as the values of a specific religion, but as shared across religions and secular values. These organisations, however, also highlighted that more can be done here. Unless the organisation was itself religious, our interlocutors only discussed the issue of religion when asked. Even here, not

90  *Religion in International Aid and Humanitarianism*

all faith-based organisations mentioned religion unless prompted. All our interviewees stressed that they did not discuss religion with their beneficiaries unless the clients themselves raised it. The main reasons given for not broaching religion included the need to remain neutral and impartial, and religion being seen as inherently subjective; the view and experience that discussions of religion amongst groups of displaced people can be harmful, exacerbating conflict and tension amongst different groups within the refugee community; and, related, the perception that religious actors, identities, and narratives can be unpredictable, with both positive and negative consequences.

Within these responses from our interlocutors, we can detect resonances of the dominant assumptions about religion, discussed in Chapter 1. At the same time, there is also an awareness that developing greater knowledge and capacity regarding religion in relation to MHPSS for people on the move is important for supporting their overall well-being. Given the relatively recent shift in approach towards religion, spirituality, and MHPSS for people on the move, there is still much research to be done. This will be an exciting and innovative field to watch in the coming years.

## Conclusion

Religion matters in international development and humanitarianism. This point has already been largely agreed on by scholars and policymakers working at the intersection of religion and development. Yet there is still much about this complex phenomenon in relation to development and humanitarianism that we do not fully appreciate or understand. This chapter has demonstrated how applying a critical intersectional framework for understanding religion enables us to identify religion's entanglement with diverse development and humanitarian issues and identify possibilities for partnership and engagement that may otherwise have been missed. It has also highlighted the mistakes that can occur when researchers and policymakers fail to either consider religion at all or only adopt a reductionist simplistic approach to how it manifests. Addressing these shortcomings cannot be separated from also addressing the underlying power inequalities on which the sector is based, which are also entangled with secularist logic. A move away from notions of "development" towards partnership, cooperation, and mutual learning would facilitate greater ownership by local communities, as well as remind donor governments and agencies that those problems we currently label as "development" are in fact global challenges for all communities everywhere.

# Notes

1 United Nations Relief and Works Agency for Palestine Refugees in the Near East.
2 The research partnership has resulted in several projects over the years with a team of researchers from Groningen as well as MM staff, including Brenda Bartelink, Christoph Grüll, Shireen Azam, Roos Feringa, Ton Groeneweg, Mieke Bakx, Stephanie Joubert, Janneke Stegeman, and Eva Krah.
3 Elsewhere (Wilson 2022a), I argue that secularism also contributes to this hierarchical binary. Its emphasis on human reason reinforces and strengthens the separation of nature and humanity, implying an understanding of nature as a resource for human beings to use or enjoy, or as a threat that must be controlled and tamed.
4 A second Moana Declaration was issued in 2013 as an outcome of the Pacific Islands Parliamentarians conference, but this declaration contains a broader focus on "population and development", incorporating attention for gender equality, gender-based violence, sexual and reproductive health, education, healthcare and sexual health, migration, sanitation, poverty reduction and infrastructure investment, alongside attention for climate change.
5 Our research team included Dr Vivienne Matthies-Boon and Patrick Landwehr.

# 5 Myths of Equality and Neutrality

## Religion in Human Rights, Law, and Public Life

In January 2021, the South Australia Civil and Administrative Tribunal (SACAT) reviewed an application for registration as an incorporated association made by the Church of the Flying Spaghetti Monster (CFSM). The CFSM first emerged in 2005 after the publication of an open letter to the Kansas School Board raising concerns about teaching Intelligent Design alongside evolution in public schools (CFSM 2022). It has quickly gained multiple followers across numerous countries around the world. Pastafarians (the name given to members of the CFSM) engage in numerous rituals and manifestations of their religion, including wearing colanders on their heads (O'Grady 2018; see Figure 5.1) and dressing as pirates (CFSM 2022).

Pastafarians have applied for legal recognition as a religion in many countries, with little success. Legal recognition in the Australian context would allow the Church to, among other things, establish formal legal rules and regulations, accountability structures, gain tax exempt status, and offer charitable social services. However, SACAT rejected the application for formal legal recognition, declaring that Pastafarianism was a "hoax religion", designed to "satirise or mock established religions" (Keane 2021), a position consistent with rulings in other contexts regarding whether the CFSM constitutes a religion or not (see, for example, Raad van State 2018; Brzozowski 2021). The ruling was a deep disappointment to Pastafarians, who believe that the Church is misunderstood. A core group of people really believe in Pastafarianism and its potential to change people's lives for the better (Keane 2021; CFSM 2022).

Two fundamental questions emerge from this case, which are central to any dilemma regarding religion, human rights, law, and public life:

1 What constitutes religion? and
2 Who gets to decide?

DOI: 10.4324/9781003037057-5

*Religion in Human Rights, Law, and Public Life* 93

*Figure 5.1* Members of the CFSM, Milan, Italy, 2012.
Source: © G.dallorto, Used with permission.

Tanya Watkins, a captain in the Australian CFSM, argued that the Church was formed for a "religious, educational, charitable or benevolent purpose" (quoted in Keane 2021), the language used in South Australia's Associations Incorporation Act to describe the kinds of organisations eligible for incorporation. The CFSM places strong emphasis on helping others, she claimed, and engages in multiple community outreach and charity initiatives. She argued that Pastafarian

## 94 *Religion in Human Rights, Law, and Public Life*

texts, which can be controversial and confronting, are used to educate and generate curiosity. Consequently, Watkins maintained that the CFSM met the criteria laid out in the Incorporation Act.

SACAT disagreed, or more accurately, Senior SACAT member Kathleen McEvoy disagreed. McEvoy explained the SACAT ruling in the following way:

> *It is* <u>my view</u> *that the Pastafarian texts can only be read as parody or satire, namely,* <u>an imitation of work made for comic effect.</u> *In* <u>my view</u>, *its purpose is to satirise or mock established religions, and it does so without discrimination... <u>I am satisfied</u> that the proposed incorporated association merely presents as having a religious purpose, but is a sham religion or a parody of religion... It was not formed for a religious purpose. On this basis, to conclude it is eligible for incorporation as a body with a religious purpose could clearly not be a preferable decision.*
>
> (quoted in Keane 2021, emphasis added)

There are at least three different understandings of what constitutes a religion mixed up in the SACAT/CFSM example, that of Watkins from the CFSM, McEvoy from SACAT, and the text in the South Australian Associations Incorporation Act, the law on which formal legal recognition of something as "religion" is based. Indeed, Watkins and McEvoy rely on the same definition in the Incorporation Act to make their contradictory arguments. Watkins emphasised the charitable acts of the CFSM and their use of the Church's texts for education. McEvoy, in contrast, appears to rely on a negative definition of religion. In the ruling she argues that the CFSM was not formed for a "religious purpose", but does not explain what a "religious purpose" is. Rather, McEvoy states that the purpose of the CFSM is to satirise established religions, though, again, not making clear what it is that makes these established religions "religion".

The consequences of denying the CFSM application for incorporation in South Australia, while disappointing for Watkins and the community she represented, did not curtail the activities of the Church and its followers in South Australia to a great extent. It may be tempting to see this case and think "what does it matter if the CFSM is denied incorporation status? What does it matter if SACAT decides they aren't a true religion?"

The CFSM case points to crucial aspects of religion's intersection with international human rights, law, and public life that have real, lived consequences for the realisation of people's rights and freedoms

*Religion in Human Rights, Law, and Public Life* 95

around the world. First, it shows that state authorities and their appointed representatives decide what counts as "religion". Such a situation should already give us pause for thought, given that a core foundational element of so-called secular states and the modern states-system is that states are supposedly neutral when it comes to matters of religion. Second, while there are legislative acts that set out criteria that communities and groups must meet in order to be recognised as a religion, often whether a community receives that recognition or not comes down to the individual interpretation of lawyers, judges, and others in positions of legal power and authority. In the CFSM case, it was Kathleen McEvoy who determined ("In my view") that the CFSM was established for the purposes of satire, not "a religious purpose". In such cases, individual lawyers, judges, and other legal and political authorities like Ms McEvoy base their understanding of religion on broader public ideas, assumptions, culture, and history of the society in which they are embedded as well as their own personal notions, yet without explicitly articulating the underlying assumptions about what "religion" is (Sullivan 2005; Berger 2018). As the case of the CFSM in South Australia highlights, different understandings of religion can operate within the same cultural, historical, political, and legal context. Such differences are magnified once we begin to consider cross-cultural and cross-contextual encounters around "religion" that we see in international politics and foreign policy, as we will examine further below. Finally, while the case of the CFSM in South Australia had little impact on the realisation of the rights and freedoms of the Church's members, as we will see through discussions of other cases in this chapter, from Pakistan, Indonesia, India, Switzerland, Italy, Germany, and Australia, differences in how "religion" is understood and how that understanding shapes the regulation of religion in public life can have real, dire consequences for people's everyday lives. An appreciation for these consequences is essential when analysing and formulating foreign policy priorities on human rights and international law.

This chapter applies the critical intersectional framework for analysing religion in international politics to the specific issue area of human rights, law, and public life. While human rights as a topic forms an important component of the development and humanitarianism agenda that we considered in the previous chapter, it is also a key focus of much foreign policy and international diplomacy on its own. The right to freedom of religion or belief (FoRB) has become a significant independent portfolio within numerous foreign ministries over recent decades (Grüll and Wilson 2018). Consequently, this chapter examines religion's relationship with human rights across multiple settings and the insights that

## 96   *Religion in Human Rights, Law, and Public Life*

can be gleaned through the application of the critical intersectional approach. As we have seen, "religion" means different things to different people in different contexts. Failure to take these diverse connotations into account can significantly impede efforts to promote recognition and implementation of human rights and dignity worldwide.

The chapter examines four issues at the nexus of religion, human rights, law, and public life, all with implications for public and foreign policy. It begins by taking up the recent surge of interest in the right to FoRB across both scholarly and policy sectors. Following this discussion, the chapter then considers the issues of minority rights and indigenous rights, drawing on cases from Pakistan and Australia. For both minority communities and Indigenous peoples, the category of "religion" in law has been particularly problematic, with significant detrimental impacts for their rights and freedoms. In most instances, this is a direct consequence of the colonial legacies and inequalities that continue to impact both domestic and international politics. Finally, the chapter explores recent developments regarding the regulation of religion in public spaces in so-called secular states and their consequences for minority religions within states as well as for efforts to promote FoRB and human rights in foreign policy and diplomacy.

A central point that emerges from these four topics is how interpretations of "religion" in law and human rights policy and practice often reflect broader power inequalities between majority and minority communities, and between states and individuals. The majority understanding of what "religion" is informs decisions that are made regarding what counts as religion and what does not, as well as the best ways to uphold and protect the rights, dignity, and freedom of diverse groups and individuals, often with contradictory outcomes and with little regard for contextual specifics and nuances, or for the perspectives and aspirations of the communities themselves.

### Context

Before commencing these discussions, it is important that we examine the context in which these discussions about religion, law, and human rights take place, and unpack the actors, identities, and narratives that are significant for understanding the category of religion (see Figures 5.2 and 5.3 for summaries for visual summaries of this).

First, it is useful to consider what we mean when we talk about human rights. According to Freeman (2017, 8), the field of human rights is dominated by lawyers, because the field itself has become a "technical, legal discourse". Yet, human rights are not only legal articles.

*Religion in Human Rights, Law, and Public Life* 97

They are also normative philosophical principles and modes of political engagement. That international human rights exist at all is the result of political, rather than legal, processes. Changes in legal protections of rights over time have largely taken place after social and political upheaval (think of suffragettes campaigning for women's right to vote, the civil rights act in the US; Indigenous people's enfranchisement in Australia; ending apartheid in South Africa; the fall of communism and the Velvet Revolution (Forsythe 2000)). Human rights are inherently political, perhaps even more so than they are legal (Freeman 2017). This raises a significant point about the nature of law that is important to bear in mind throughout the discussions in this chapter. It is common to think about law as a neutral arbiter of conflicts between different groups in society. Yet law is a codification of social and cultural norms and practices. Rather than being neutral, law reflects the moral values and standards that inform how a society functions (Berger 2018). Changes in law tend to follow changes in society and politics, not the other way around (Berger 2018). Further, law is always made, applied, and enforced by someone, meaning that law is not only a reflection of the moral values and norms that inform a society. Law is also a reflection of the values and norms of the most powerful groups in a society. This is the case whether we are speaking of national or international law.

As well as being political and legal, human rights are social, in that determining what human rights mean and how they should be interpreted is an ongoing process of negotiation and interaction amongst multiple stakeholders, including inter-governmental organisations (IGOs), non-governmental organisations (NGOs), states, lawyers, politicians, corporations, and individual rights bearers themselves. This points to a further dimension, that human rights are lived and experienced (Freeman 2017, 6). Human rights are constantly evolving, at the same time as they provide us with foundational standards for how human beings should be treated by one another and by the institutions that societies have collectively developed at the national and international level.

The collective development of human rights standards and institutions, particularly within international law and politics, forms another central component of the context in which we analyse religion's relationship with human rights and law. Human rights are plagued by ongoing and arguably irresolvable debates about their origins, whether they are in fact "universal" or a cultural artefact of Europe and North America imposed on the rest of the world. Supporters and advocates of international human rights point to historical antecedents of modern human rights from across time and space, across cultures, religions, political systems, geographies, and economies to demonstrate that human rights are indeed "natural", "inalienable", "universal" (see, for example, Ishay 2008; Adami 2012; Donnelly 2013). Yet equally ardent sceptics and opponents of the human rights project will point to the domination of international institutions and drafting committees by "Western" and Western-educated elites; the colonial regimes still in place when the Universal Declaration of Human Rights and other international human rights legal architecture were signed and ratified; and the ongoing inequalities of power as similarly compelling evidence that human rights are a Euro-American neo-imperial construct, perhaps most clearly articulated as part of the "Asian Values" debate in the mid-1990s (Merry 2006). For the purposes of this chapter, and arguably for any analysis of international human rights, it is important not to be distracted by this debate over whether human

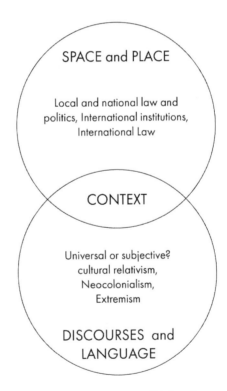

*Figure 5.2* The Context of Religion, Human Rights, Law and Public Life.
Image Credit: Jessica Mills Designs.

## Religion in Human Rights, Law, and Public Life 99

rights are universal or culturally specific. While this is a frequent point of contention in international politics, it is arguably driven by political and ideological commitments, and consequently is unlikely to ever be resolved. The main point when it comes to human rights is not their origin or their historical development. Rather, it is the fact that the international community *now* agrees that human rights, however imperfect, are important, and commits to upholding these standards. Subsequently, for analysing religion's relationship with human rights, law, and public life, what matters is when, how, and by whom arguments regarding the universality or cultural relativism of human rights are made and how the category of religion is invoked in such claims.

### Actors

There is a multiplicity of actors to consider when analysing religion's intersection with human rights, law, and public life. Religious actors encompass individual rights bearers making claims regarding their religious practices (Tanya Watkins from the CFSM, for example), but also religious communities – groups who congregate around particular institutions, beliefs, or rituals, or who are identified as a religious community by others based on historical, cultural, economic, or ethnic factors and characteristics. The identification of communities as "religious" points to another significant group of actors involved when it comes to analysing religion, law, and human rights – those with the power to designate what is and is not "religion", namely, lawyers, judges, political representatives, but also scholars of religion who research, publish, and may even be called on as expert witnesses for legal hearings. These actors may or may not identify as "religious" themselves and if they do would likely maintain that their personal religious identity is separate from their professional identity and role (their private versus their public persona). Like development and humanitarianism, there is also a vast array of NGOs and FBOs involved in advocacy and campaigning on human rights and religion, all with diverse priorities and agendas, working with local communities on the ground to support them to claim their rights, as well as advocating for greater action and protection of rights at the inter-governmental level.

### Identities

Identities are crucial to make explicit when analysing religion in relation to law and human rights. This is because violations and denials of the right to FoRB, for example, or notions of FoRB as conflicting with women's rights or the rights of LGBTQI+ people are often based on the religious identity of particular groups, whether that identity is self-proclaimed or ascribed by others. In the same way as assumptions are made about the religious identity of people seeking asylum based on their country of origin, as we saw in Chapter 4, particular characteristics are ascribed by political and legal authorities to individuals and communities when it comes to religion, law, and human rights that then materially affect whether their rights are realised. As we shall see in the case of Muslims in India, religion is not the only identifying characteristic the members of this community share. They are also often poor and economically and politically disenfranchised, sharing similar ethnic origins and cultural practices. Yet they are primarily identified based on their religion by political authorities in India, with specific consequences for how they are treated.

## Narratives

Religious narratives play a particularly important role in navigating some of the debates and discourses that affect international human rights noted above. Because of their association with "Western"/

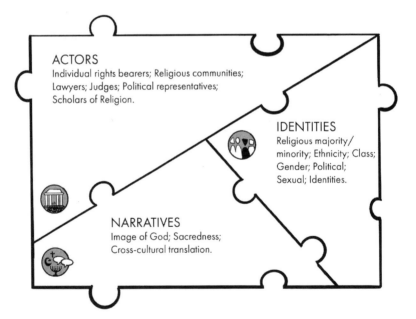

*Figure 5.3* Actors, Identities, and Narratives in Religion, Human Rights, Law, and Public Life.
Image Credit: Jessica Mills Designs.

*Religion in Human Rights, Law, and Public Life* 101

neo-colonial agendas, the language of human rights in some contexts may be ineffective or may even actively hinder efforts to promote dignity and respect for rights in different communities. Religious actors, NGOs, and FBOs instead utilise particular narratives, such as the sacredness of all human beings, as a way to vernacularise the language of rights in a way that is relevant for the specific context in which they are working (Wilson 2011; 2022b). We will see different examples of this throughout the cases we consider in the remainder of this chapter.

## The Right to Freedom of Religion or Belief

Debate over the right to FoRB has intensified in academic and policy circles in recent years. This intensification is partially a response to increasing attention for FoRB by government departments, particularly the perceived increase in what some scholars refer to as "American-style" religious freedom influencing global policy and NGO agendas (Hurd 2015). While multiple positions, perspectives, and approaches exist on the question of the right to FoRB, these tend to fall somewhere along a spectrum between those who believe FoRB is a universal inalienable right that should be upheld and protected at all times and in all places ("defenders" of FoRB) (Grim and Finke 2011; Hertzke 2012; Philpott 2013; Philpott and Shah 2016, 383) and those who view the right to FoRB as "impossible", for multiple reasons ("critics" of FoRB) (Sullivan 2005; Mahmood and Danchin 2014; Hurd 2015; Mahmood 2016). While there are numerous approaches to FoRB between these two ends of the spectrum, for the purposes of this discussion, I focus on the differences between defenders and critics.

The disagreements between these two positions are shaped by and reflect the broader tensions around understanding "religion" and the international discourses on human rights outlined above. A third important aspect of this disagreement is the question of whether rights in general, and FoRB in particular, apply to individuals or communities. In the context of FoRB, this tension is exacerbated by competing understandings of the concept of religion. In European and North American contexts, "religion or belief" is often understood in an internal, cognitive sense, as the right of an individual to choose to believe or not in a particular set of doctrinal principles or creeds. This cognitive understanding of "religion or belief" is not always consistent with concepts, understandings, and practices of "religion" in areas outside the so-called "West". Amongst some communities in India and Indonesia, as we shall briefly explore, "religion" is frequently understood as communal identity, as belonging to a particular group. This belonging may be based on family, culture, birth, and upbringing rather than an

102 *Religion in Human Rights, Law, and Public Life*

(optional) intellectual decision to believe or not. In such contexts, an individual may have multiple "religious" affiliations, in the sense that they may be culturally "Muslim", for example, but their individual beliefs may be atheist or Christian (Mahmood 2016). This adds significant complication to understandings and applications of the right to FoRB.

A significant dimension of international discourses and disagreements around FoRB is the transatlantic distinction in the language and conceptualisation of this right. In the US, the right is often expressed as the right to "religious freedom" or "religious liberty", whereas Canada, European countries, and the European Union have been careful to express the right as the right to "freedom of religion or belief". Important historical antecedents contribute to understanding this distinction in language. The so-called religious wars in Europe and the narrative of the founding of the US by people fleeing religious persecution in Europe seeking to establish a "new world" that would be a shining example of religious pluralism and tolerance to the old world are significant (Cherry 1998). The spectre of religious violence and intolerance so influenced the establishment of modern states in Europe, so the story goes, that the principle of the right to FoRB is understood implicitly as freedom *from* religion or belief in the European context (Asch 1997; Mavelli 2011). In the US, by contrast, the right became conceptualised in the positive sense as freedom *to* believe whatever one wished. Both narratives are obviously flawed. The so-called wars of religion in Europe were less about doctrinal disagreements (evidenced by alliances between Catholic and Protestant states during the conflict) and more about the struggle between ecclesiastical and monarchical authorities for control over territory and resources (Asch 1997; Mavelli 2011; Wilson 2012). In the US, the new colony was not as tolerant of divergent beliefs as it is often remembered to be (Cherry 1998). Nonetheless, these narratives play a powerful role in different assumptions and discourses around the right to FoRB in the contemporary transatlantic political landscape.

Some actors within global politics also see the language of "religious freedom" in the US and as part of US foreign policy as "Christianity by stealth" (Castelli 2007), an association that contributes to scepticism of and suspicion towards any efforts to promote or advocate for FoRB, as we will see in the examples we explore below. This association is not unwarranted, since the precursors to what eventually became international religious freedom law in the US were primarily focused on the rights and freedoms of Christians around the world (Petersen 2021). Owing to this history, European actors have sought to

*Religion in Human Rights, Law, and Public Life* 103

distance themselves from "religious freedom" and instead adopt the term "FoRB". The right to FoRB as expressed in Article 18 of the Universal Declaration of Human Rights encompasses not just religion, but also freedom of thought and conscience. As such, this right arguably encompasses not just "religious" beliefs, but political and philosophical beliefs and values. The shorthand of "religious freedom" or even "religion or belief" at times obscures this important aspect.

These distinctions between "religious freedom" and "freedom of religion or belief", as important as they are in the transatlantic context, matter less in broader global political conversations around the right to FoRB. Whether using "religious freedom" or "FoRB", the connotation is the same for many actors external to Europe and North America. Consequently, efforts to promote FoRB in foreign policy are met with the same level of scepticism and resistance as "religious freedom" in some quarters, seen as subterfuge for Christian evangelism, a Western neo-colonial imposition, and/or an effort to dilute the beliefs and practices of different religious communities. The increasing restrictions on the wearing of symbols such as headscarves, burkinis, turbans, and other manifestations of religion in public settings in Europe (explored in more detail below) suggest a double standard between European domestic and foreign policy on FoRB, reinforcing the idea that "FoRB" or "religious freedom" in US and European foreign policy really means "the promotion of Christianity". These attitudes are evident in the examples from Cirebon and Gujarat considered below.

Alongside the colonial history that contributes to suspicious responses to FoRB promotion, the recent surge in attention for FoRB by Western powers has formed part of a wider package of policy initiatives under the label of "countering violent extremism" (CVE). FoRB is presented here as something of an antidote to conflict and violent extremism (e.g. Grim and Finke 2011; Henne, Hudgins and Shah 2012). Yet Mandaville and Nozell (2017) note that CVE has the potential to proscribe certain kinds of beliefs and practices and consequently restrict individual rights to FoRB, a situation that has arisen in relation to the Rohingya in Myanmar, as we saw in Chapter 3, but also the Uyghurs in China (Kam and Clarke 2021). CVE initiatives are predominantly directed towards Muslim populations within Western contexts and towards Muslim-majority countries. As such, the renewed interest in FoRB as part of this swathe of policies is viewed with suspicion by some governments and civil society actors. This does not mean that these actors are hostile to the value of respecting diversity and difference that sits at the core of FoRB. What occurs instead is that actors translate or "vernacularise" (Merry 2006; Wilson 2022b) the

104   *Religion in Human Rights, Law, and Public Life*

right to FoRB into language, concepts, and approaches that resonate and make sense relevant to the specific context in which they work, as we will see in the examples from Cirebon and Gujarat discussed below. In this section, I draw on material collected during interviews our Groningen-based research team carried out in 2015 with members of local organisations partnering with Mensen met een Missie to promote the right to FoRB, as part of a project funded by the Dutch foreign ministry.

## Promoting FoRB in Indonesia and India

In Cirebon, Indonesia, members of local organisation Fahmina (who we met in Chapter 4; see also Figure 5.4) commented during interviews that promoting FoRB in the Indonesian context is complicated by the emphasis on religious plurality and diversity that often accompanies such efforts. Reference to terms such as "freedom", "religion", and "belief" is likely to trigger misunderstandings and tensions. For example, where "freedom" in relation to FoRB arguably refers to individual choice of religion and entails individual expression of this freedom, promoting pluralism and diversity in Cirebon is viewed by some community members with suspicion. In this context, "freedom of religion" is understood as promoting a plurality of beliefs *within* a religious community or tradition and thereby diluting the purity of the tradition, rather than a plurality and diversity of the different communities themselves. Social cohesion and stability, for many community members, are a matter of religious conformity in terms of both belief and practice. Promoting pluralism and diversity as an individual choice is considered contradictory and disruptive to this social cohesion and stability (Grüll and Wilson 2018, 96). Interviewees described a need to "break down" the language of FoRB to make it more accessible and usable. Activists from Fahmina do this through applying locally embedded concepts instead, following on from Fahmina's overarching interpretation that "human rights are about becoming fully human, being good to yourself and to others" (Grüll and Wilson 2018, 96). Specifically, *Ngaji Rasa* (I am you, you are me) and *Silaturahmi* (gathering) feature prominently in Fahmina's approach, because these concepts and principles are also deeply embedded in everyday life in Cirebon. They reflect Fahmina's emphasis on building relationships across socially constructed divides (such as religious identities) through direct encounter and through recognising the shared humanity in one another.

*Figure 5.4* Dr. Faqihuddin Abdul Kodir speaking at a Gender Equality and Diversity gathering organised by Fahmina Institute, Cirebon, Indonesia.
Source: Mensen met een Missie.

Similarly, in Gujarat, India, staff and volunteers working on a FoRB project described during interviews how they changed all references to the project to "Alliance for Justice and Peace" (AJP). The term "belief" is almost never used in India, because, according to the interviewees, "belief" is associated with superstitions like black magic and is thus unhelpful to mention in the field. They discuss "religion" internally within the organisation but do not mention "religion" at all externally. Mentioning religion, according to AJP, is counter-productive and risky as a result of the politically fuelled tensions around religious identities and diverse religious communities and has the potential to undermine their goal of improving the situation for religious minorities. Instead, AJP utilises the concept of *uthna-baithna* (literally "getting up-sitting down") to place emphasis on the importance of building relationships. In their activities, AJP focus on issues of shared concern within communities, such as food, sanitation, healthcare, education, and employment, issues that are not directly or explicitly connected with religious identity, yet where discrimination based on religious identity may be endemic (Grüll and Wilson 2018, 97).

This emphasis on issues of shared concern reflects a broader strategic choice by AJP to focus their work on the general group of "people

106    *Religion in Human Rights, Law, and Public Life*

excluded from development", rather than on specific religious minorities and violations of the right to FoRB. AJP are aware that discrimination and exclusion of people from development projects and access to other human rights often takes place based on religious identity. Yet explicitly focusing on FoRB and religious identity generates more hostility and opposition from the surrounding community than focusing on the exclusion of people from economic, social, cultural, and political development. To have a higher chance of increasing people's economic and political inclusion, AJP focus on addressing the symptoms of this discrimination, rather than its root causes. Interview participants from the Muslim community in Gujarat voiced opposition to openly asserting injustice against the Muslim minority and solely asking for recognition of their rights, saying "Relations are everything, asking for rights will only lead to conflict". Implicit in this statement is the ongoing power imbalance between the Muslim minority and Hindu majority – the Muslim community have to "ask" for their rights from the Hindu majority. From their perspective, to avoid conflict, it is better to maintain relations. A challenge in approaching the pursuit of rights in this way is that it does not address the underlying problems of inequality between different communities. While some aspects of the lives of religious, particularly Muslim, minorities in Gujarat may be materially improved in the short term, they will continue to exist precariously at the margins of society unless and until the more fundamental issue of discrimination based on religious identity can be addressed (Grüll and Wilson 2018). This is not to suggest that AJP should approach the problem differently. Their strategy is directly informed by the desires and perspectives of the community with which they work, thereby privileging the needs and priorities of the community themselves, rather than the priorities of international donors. The point is rather to highlight the very significant challenges and dilemmas faced by activists and advocates, the choices open to them and that, whichever choice they make, there will be both advances and setbacks when it comes to the realisation of rights in the everyday lives of people in the communities in which they work.

## Minority Rights

The situation in Gujarat points to another significant challenge when it comes to the intersection of religion, law, and human rights – the rights of minority communities. The right to FoRB is often posited as a means to advocate for and protect the rights of minority communities who are identified primarily by a religious designation. As

*Religion in Human Rights, Law, and Public Life* 107

Hurd (2015) and Mahmood (2016) have pointed out, promoting FoRB in foreign policy and international diplomacy as a method for reducing inter-religious conflict and tension can have the opposite effect. Traditions that are acknowledged and identified as "religions" within the international community may not be recognised as such in specific national locations. Most national constitutional articles that reference the right to FoRB include a variation of the following clauses: that every citizen has the right to profess and practise their religion, *subject to law, public order, and morality.* As Nelson (2020b) highlights, this clause provides sufficient room for interpretation to allow governments to determine that the beliefs of certain groups or minorities "disrupt public order" and can therefore legitimately and legally be restricted. An emphasis on FoRB can foster heightened attention and sensitivity to religious identity, making religious minorities more of a target for violence, rather than less (Hurd 2015; Mahmood 2016). Consequently, promoting the right to FoRB for minorities may reinforce their difference and otherness, making them more vulnerable, rather than upholding their dignity and humanity and providing them with greater protection.

Nelson (2020b) discusses the example of the Ahmadiyya community in Pakistan to demonstrate the lived realities of these ambiguities around FoRB and the rights of minority groups. The Ahmadiyya community follow the teachings of Ghulam Ahmad, a 19th-century man from Punjab who the Ahmadiyya consider a prophet in the Muslim tradition after the Prophet Muhammad. The Ahmadiyya consider themselves to be part of the broader Muslim community (Nelson 2020b). This membership of the broader Muslim tradition, however, is questioned, not recognised, or outright rejected by others from outside the Ahmadiyya community. Indeed, there are some within the broader Muslim community who see the Ahmadiyya as blasphemous, because in their view Muhammad was the last and greatest of the prophets (Saeed 2016; Nelson 2020b).

The Ahmadiyya are a minority community within Sunni Muslim-majority Pakistan. The question of whether the Ahmadiyya are or are not "Muslim" has been the source of significant political and civil tension, violence, and unrest since the post-colonial formation of the Pakistani state (Saeed 2016; Nelson 2020b). According to Nelson (2020b), the article on the right to FoRB as expressed in the Pakistan constitution originated in the Constitution of the Irish Republic, migrating essentially verbatim to Pakistan via India. Yet the interpretation of this article within the Pakistan legal context has increasingly shifted over recent decades to privilege the maintenance of public order over

108 *Religion in Human Rights, Law, and Public Life*

and above the right of the Ahmadiyya to practise their religion. This legal reinterpretation has been driven by a largely political response to public rioting and fundamentally privileges the rights of the majority over the rights of the minority.

Since the 1970s, the predominantly peaceful practices of the Ahmadiyya have been increasingly targeted and restricted as sources of public disorder. Specifically, two constitutional reforms were introduced that restricted the ability of the Ahmadiyya to participate in the politics and public life of Pakistan. The first of these was introduced in 1973, requiring that each president and prime minister swear an oath not only that they are Muslim, but also that they believe that Muhammad was the last of the prophets. This requirement makes it virtually impossible for members of the Ahmadiyya community to become head of state without compromising their beliefs, commitments, and identity. A second constitutional reform followed one year later in 1974, amending Article 260 of the Pakistani constitution to specifically state that to be "Muslim" in Pakistan means a person who "does not believe in or recognize as a prophet or religious reformer, any person who claimed or claims to be a prophet... after Muhammad" (quoted in Nelson 2020b, 142). The wording of the amendment suggests that the Ahmadiyya were the specific targets of this reform. These constitutional amendments were the catalysts for the shift in legal interpretations in Pakistan that increasingly privileged the majority Sunni Muslim position over the rights and protections of the Ahmadiyya community (Nelson 2020b).

Before the 1980s, Pakistani courts ruled that the Ahmadiyya had the right to worship, pray, and practise their religion. The Ahmadiyya had been cast in public and legal discourse as victims of vigilante conservative Muslim violence. Yet after the constitutional reforms of the 1970s and a series of committee rulings and other political developments, during the 1980s, the Ahmadiyya were increasingly portrayed as provocateurs, deliberately antagonising the majority religious community (Nelson 2020b). Subsequently, Pakistan courts and parliamentary legislation have determined that the Ahmadiyya practices present a threat to public order, because of the violent reactions from the rest of the Muslim community (Nelson 2020b). The Ahmadiyya community have thus been increasingly restricted in their ability to publicly practise their religion in Pakistan (Saeed 2016).

Numerous other examples exist within international politics of minorities whose claim for protection based on religious identity and FoRB has contributed to making them more vulnerable rather than less. Hurd (2015) highlights the situation of the Alevis in Turkey, while Mahmood (2016) demonstrates similar dynamics taking place for Coptic Christians in Egypt. This is not to suggest that these groups are not entitled to the

*Religion in Human Rights, Law, and Public Life* 109

right to FoRB. Rather, we must be aware of the implications that advocacy and activism based on the right to FoRB may have in contexts where the very basis of the claim to the right to FoRB – the "religion" and "religious" identity of the minorities concerned – is questioned, not recognised at all, or presented as a deliberate act of political disruption by legal and political authorities. In these situations, other strategies, such as advocating for the right to non-discrimination (Article 2 of the Universal Declaration of Human Rights), may be more effective than promoting attention for the right to FoRB (Grüll and Wilson 2018).

## Indigenous Rights

The political and legal distinction between "religion" and "non-religion" has also been a crucial aspect of Indigenous peoples' fight to protect their traditional lands and practices in settler colonial states. In both the US and Australia, for example, Indigenous peoples have continually had to navigate and negotiate the categories of "religious" and "secular" in law to be granted permission by legal and political authorities to continue observing some of their traditional practices and maintain ownership of traditional lands (Maddox 2010; Wenger 2011). The power imbalance between Indigenous peoples and settler colonial governments regarding religion thus occurs at two levels: first, in that Indigenous peoples have had to struggle and fight to maintain their rituals, traditions, and practices; and, second, in that they have had to do so through the language, systems, and categories of knowledge of white settler colonial powers (also largely codified in international law) and not within their own frameworks of meaning making. Such cases may initially appear purely domestic and thus irrelevant to IR. Yet the rights of Indigenous peoples is increasingly recognised as a transnational political issue. In the context of growing concerns about climate change, threats to Indigenous communities' heritage and sacred sites from corporations, and the navigation of relationships between traditional owners and nation-states as inheritors of colonial era power (Conway 2013), the rights of Indigenous peoples are increasingly significant for IR. Countless examples of these challenges for Indigenous peoples exist from all over the world. Here I examine the Hindmarsh Island case from Australia to draw out the specific challenges that exist for Indigenous peoples to voice their spiritualities and claim their rights within domestic and international rights language embedded within European legal and philosophical traditions. (Indigenous Australian readers are advised that the following section contains references to persons who are now deceased.)

The Hindmarsh Island controversy arose in the early 1990s in relation to the proposed building of the Hindmarsh-Goolwa Bridge (see Figure 5.5) in South Australia. In 1994, a group of Ngarrindjeri female elders, led by Dr Doreen Kartinyeri, lodged a claim under the Commonwealth Aboriginal and Torres Strait Islander Heritage Protection Act to prevent the building of the bridge. The basis of their claim was that building the bridge would fatally affect the reproductive capacity of Ngarrindjeri women and the broader cosmos. In Ngarrindjeri tradition, they hold that nothing must come between the waters around Hindmarsh Island (known as Kumarangk in Ngarrindjeri language) and the sky, otherwise Ngarrindjeri women will become sick and this will affect their reproductive capacity (Maddox 2010, 13). Knowledge about the reproductivity of the community and its relationship to the cosmos was restricted to a select group of women with the necessary "skills, sensitivity and receptivity" to intuit this relationship, who then passed their knowledge down through the generations (Weiner 2002, 53). Kartinyeri stated that when she was a young girl, her Aunty Rosie had told her about the women's initiation rituals that took place at Kumarangk (Kartinyeri and Anderson 2008, 18). Kartinyeri held it as her sacred duty to protect not only the place but the rules around who could and could not be permitted to have knowledge about what occurred there (Keyzer 2020). The tightly protected nature of this knowledge for the Ngarrindjeri people meant that its precise nature and details could not be publicly disclosed, and particularly could not be revealed to men.

*Figure 5.5* The Hindmarsh-Goolwa Bridge.
Source: Andrew McMillan, Wikimedia/public domain.

*Religion in Human Rights, Law, and Public Life* 111

To appreciate the sacredness of Kumarangk (Hindmarsh Island) for Ngarrindjeri women, these statements need to be considered within the broader context of Indigenous Australian spiritualities. Many of the Indigenous clans and communities that inhabit the Australian continent view the relationship between people and land as continuous and holistic. Land and nature are not separated from humans, objects for ownership and use, as they are understood within European-influenced political and legal frameworks. Rather, land, sea, and sky are dynamic, integral parts of Indigenous Australian communities, relationships, and spirituality (Povinelli 1995). This intimate relationship with the landscape comes from the "Dreaming", a collective term used to refer to Indigenous Australian understandings of their origins. According to Galarrwuy Yunupingu (1996), the "Dreaming" is primarily "a word we [Indigenous Australians] learned to use for the ears of white people for the sake of communication". Each Indigenous language group (of which there are currently more than 250, with over 800 dialects[1]) has its own term for referring to this era (Mikhailovich et al. 2011, 8). During the "Dreaming", ancestral spirit beings emerged from the then formless earth and assumed the shapes and identities of beings that now constitute the humans, animals, and plants present in the world today (Mikhailovich et al. 2011). As they travelled across the earth, hunting, eating, dancing, and fighting, their activities shaped the mountains, rivers, deserts, forests, and other features of the landscape that are present today. While the events of the "Dreaming" form the origins of the world, for Indigenous Australians the "Dreaming" is not just an event that occurred in the past. Indigenous Australians have a cyclical rather than linear understanding of time (Rose 1998). Consequently, the "Dreaming" is something that every generation of Indigenous Australians experiences. The land and the spirits and ancestors that inhabit the land continue to speak to those who are alive in the present (Povinelli 1995).

Connection to the landscape is central within this meaning-making framework, because it is the source of life and well-being of the community, besides providing intimate and continual connection between present generations and their ancestors. The ongoing separation and dislocation of Indigenous Australians from their ancestral lands as a result of colonial dispossession is thus not simply a matter of inequality and injustice. It affects the physical and mental health and well-being of Indigenous Australians today (Petheram et al. 2010; Mikhailovich et al. 2011), making the ongoing damage to land from mining, development, and climate change a source of severe physical and mental distress for Indigenous Australians. Within a legal framework based on

## 112 *Religion in Human Rights, Law, and Public Life*

English and more broadly European understandings of religion and spirituality, as well as land ownership, recognition of the centrality of land for Indigenous spirituality and well-being has been and continues to be fraught with challenges, not to mention pain and anguish for Indigenous Australians.

In 1994, following the Ngarrindjeri women's claim, then federal Minister for Indigenous Affairs, Alan Tickner, implemented a 25-year ban on construction of the Hindmarsh-Goolwa Bridge, under the terms of the Heritage Protection Act. This decision was vehemently opposed by supporters of the bridge project, who pejoratively referred to the basis of the Ngarrandjeri claims as "secret women's business" (Keyzer 2020). What followed was an ugly legal and political battle, drawn out over many years, in which the Ngarrindjeri women who had submitted the claim were publicly humiliated and vilified (Keyzer 2020). Here I detail only two of at least five public inquiries, in addition to several legal cases, that took place in relation to the Kumarangk (Hindmarsh Island) controversy. It is also crucial to appreciate that the Kumarangk (Hindmarsh Island) controversy arose in a period of cultural backlash against significant advances in the acknowledgement of Indigenous rights that had occurred during the 1980s (Keyzer 2020). Colonialism, race politics, culture wars, gender inequality, historical injustice, and the nature and definition of religion and spirituality are all entangled in the contours of this case.

A separate group of female elders of the Ngarrindjeri community indicated that they had not heard about the sacred rituals (not that they did not exist, only that they had not heard of them). This statement was sufficient for some members of parliament and the media to accuse the women who had submitted the original claim of lying or fabricating the tradition for the purposes of halting the building of the bridge. The South Australian government established a Royal Commission in June 1995 to determine whether the "secret women's business" was genuine or a fabrication, and then if it were a fabrication, the extent and nature of that fabrication (Maddox 2010, 12). The women who had lodged the claim did not give evidence as witnesses at the commission, yet nonetheless the commission concluded that they had lied (Langton 1996, 211). According to the commission, the beliefs, if they existed at all, were not valid, because they could not be empirically proven or demonstrated and were not "supported by any form of logic" (Maddox 2010, 12), a highly subjective and strategic argument regarding the foundations for religious beliefs and practices, which are more often associated

*Religion in Human Rights, Law, and Public Life* 113

with irrationality and a lack of logic. Maddox (2010) suggests that this focus on the need for validity and evidence reflects a secular tendency to associate authenticity with "empirical verifiability" – because the beliefs were secret and restricted, they could not be verified and therefore the court concluded that they did not exist or were not valid if they did.

The Mathews inquiry, held in 1996, similarly focused on the claims by the Ngarrindjeri women that the building of the bridge would detrimentally impact their reproductivity. In contrast to the Royal Commission, Justice Jane Mathews, who was heading the inquiry, upheld the claim that there was in fact a genuine and long-standing tradition amongst the Ngarrindjeri people that nothing should come in between the water and the sky. However, she stopped short of upholding the ban on the bridge's construction. She determined that the prohibition on anything coming between the water and the sky was itself not a tradition but rather a rule deriving from the tradition. The reason or justification for this rule and its connection to the tradition itself were not provided. Neither was it made clear what the connection was between the rule and its consequence – that Ngarrindjeri women would become sick (Maddox 2010, 13).

What Mathews appears to have been looking for is an article of faith or belief, of doctrine, that explained *why* nothing should come between the water and sky, and *why* if something did, women would become ill. Despite the testimony of two anthropologists offered as part of the inquiry, who indicated that such justifications were unlikely to be found within any Indigenous traditions, Mathews nonetheless found insufficient grounds for upholding the ban on the construction of the Hindmarsh-Goolwa Bridge. As Maddox (2010) observes, in requiring such a systematic structure to explain the traditions and practices of the Ngarrindjeri people, Mathews was implicitly applying a Euro-Christian understanding of religion to a tradition that is so vastly different it may literally be understood as constituting a different world, operating on a different reality (Blaser 2013; Viveiros de Castro 2013; Wilson 2017). In both the Royal Commission and the Mathews' Inquiry, while they reached different conclusions regarding whether the tradition existed or not, the outcome for the Ngarrindjeri people was the same: construction of the bridge went ahead regardless of their concerns and opposition, officially opening in 2001. In 2002, the local Alexandrina council offered an apology to the Ngarrindjeri people, and in 2010 the South Australian government formally acknowledged that

114   *Religion in Human Rights, Law, and Public Life*

the "secret women's business" had not been fabricated (Guerrera 2021). While this offered some consolation for the local community and the women who had been involved in the case, it came too late for Doreen Kartinyeri, who had passed away from cancer in 2007 (Keyzer 2020).

Three crucial points emerge from this case. First, it is impossible to appreciate the significance of Kumarangk for Ngarrindjeri women's spirituality without an acknowledgement of the broader structures of indigenous Australian spirituality and the central place of relationships to landscape in that spirituality. This contextual knowledge, however, was not something that was given due consideration in the legal proceedings surrounding the Kumarangk (Hindmarsh Island) controversy. Second, and more broadly, in order to realise their rights, Indigenous peoples must constantly navigate the vague and shifting categories of secular and religion (Wenger 2011). Indigenous peoples' rituals, traditions, and practices must be made to fit within the secular (Christian) assumptions regarding what "religion" is if these customs are to either be permitted to continue or achieve recognition and legitimacy within the broader context of white settler colonial law and politics. If they cannot be adequately reconciled with either category, as in the Kumarangk (Hindmarsh Island) case, the practices are either ignored or denounced as false. Third, Indigenous peoples are continually forced to justify their rituals and traditions and claim the right to continue these practices within the context of meaning-making frameworks that do not fit or make sense with their own worldview, reinforcing their own position of inequality and marginality in both domestic and international law.

While the Kumarangk (Hindmarsh Island) controversy took place almost 30 years ago, the sacredness and spirituality of Indigenous peoples' relationship to landscape and its centrality for the physical and mental health and well-being of individuals and communities continues to be disregarded and poorly understood. In 2020, international mining company Rio Tinto destroyed a cave in Juukan Gorge, Western Australia, that showed 46,000 years of continual occupation and a 4,000 year-old genetic link to Kuramma people, the present-day traditional owners (Wahlquist 2020). The company had received ministerial permission to destroy the site in 2013 for the purposes of expanding an iron ore mine. Despite subsequent archaeological excavation revealing that the site was more than twice as old as originally thought, and regular meetings between Rio Tinto and the traditional owners, the destruction proceeded. The destruction

*Religion in Human Rights, Law, and Public Life* 115

of sacred Indigenous sites either by or for commercial industry occurs across multiple other regions of the world. At the time of writing, the office of the UN Special Rapporteur for FoRB is preparing a report on Indigenous Peoples and the right to FoRB. This report will offer even more material regarding the present-day situation for Indigenous peoples and how the complex contours of the category of "religion" in domestic and international law affect their rights claims.

## "Culture" or "Religion"? Regulating Religious Symbols in European Public Spheres

The challenges we have examined so far in this chapter, particularly minority and Indigenous rights, apart from demonstrating the shifting and indeterminate nature of what "religion" is, have also highlighted that questions about what counts as "religion" often form the site of power imbalances and inequalities between majority and minority populations. Debates about the presence of religious symbols in public life in Europe, the US, Australia, and Canada – which have increased and intensified within the last two decades – also illustrate this contestation. The regulation of religious symbols in public life connects with the different types of assumptions informing how "religion" is understood and the perceived role it should play in politics and society, mapping on to the different political secularisms discussed in Chapter 1. Regulation of religion is also inextricably entangled with other power relationships, including majority/minority, individual/state, and gender and sexuality.

Several recent cases in the European Court of Human Rights (ECtHR; see Figure 5.6) and the European Court of Justice (ECJ), amongst others, have raised questions concerning how exactly a symbol is determined to be "religious". What we can observe across a number of different contexts is that whether a symbol is interpreted as "religious" or not depends on the dominant socio-cultural and political understanding of what "religion" is, as well as which particular "religion" has been historically, culturally, and politically privileged. Lori Beaman's (2013) analysis of the *Lautsi and others v Italy* case in Europe and the Bouchard Taylor report in Canada demonstrates that symbols associated with the majority religion (Christianity in the two cases she discusses) are being classified as important parts of cultural heritage and thus permissible within the otherwise secular public sphere. This includes symbols such as crosses, crucifixes, nativity scenes, and the Ten Commandments. Other symbols associated with minority religions – such as headscarves, turbans, burkinis, and veils – are classified solely as religious, and consequently a disruptive influence within supposedly neutral secular public spaces.

A comparison of the *Lautsi* case with another ECtHR case, *Dahlab v Switzerland*, both of which concern religious symbols in public classrooms, acutely demonstrates this difference in categorisation of majority religious symbols compared to those of minority groups. It also shows the pervasive influence of social and political discourses in legal processes, reinforcing the argument that law is not neutral, but rather a codification of the norms and values of dominant groups. In *Lautsi and others v Italy*, Ms Soile Lautsi brought a case against the Italian government claiming that the presence of crucifixes on the wall of the classrooms at the public school her children attended was a violation of both her and her childrens' right to FoRB under Article 9 of the European Convention on Human Rights. Ms Lautsi had first complained unsuccessfully to the school board in 2002. Subsequently, she took her case to the local district court, and then through the various

*Figure 5.6* The Courtroom of the European Court of Human Rights, Strasbourg.
Source: Adrian Grycuk/Wikimedia.

*Religion in Human Rights, Law, and Public Life* 117

levels of the Italian court system before the hearing at the ECtHR in 2009. While the ECtHR found in Ms Lautsi's favour, the Italian government appealed the decision to the Grand Chamber of the ECtHR. In 2011, the Grand Chamber found in favour of the Italian government. The crucifix was thus allowed to remain on the wall of the public school (Beaman 2013).

There are three key points about the crucifix that the Grand Chamber makes in its ruling that are important to note for our purposes. First, they noted that the crucifix "is an essentially passive symbol" that does not violate the principle of neutrality in the classroom. Second, the Grand Chamber found that there was "no evidence ... that the display of a religious symbol on classroom walls may have an influence on pupils" (ECtHR Grand Chamber Decision 2011). Third, the Grand Chamber accepted the Italian government's argument that while the crucifix is a religious symbol, it is also an important part of Italian cultural heritage and embodies principles of democracy, equality, non-violence, and justice (ECtHR Grand Chamber Decision 2011).

These comments from the Grand Chamber regarding the nature of the crucifix are particularly striking when considered next to the ECtHR ruling in the 2001 *Dahlab v Switzerland* case, to which the Grand Chamber referred in its ruling on *Lautsi*. In the *Dahlab* case, a Swiss primary school teacher, Ms Dahlab, had converted to Islam and began wearing a headscarf while teaching. She was careful not to discuss anything about her religious beliefs with her students. If any of them did ask why she was wearing the headscarf, she told them it was to keep her ears warm. The Swiss Education Board nevertheless ordered her to remove it and refrain from wearing it while teaching because it violated the principle of denominational neutrality in the classroom (Evans 2006). Ms Dahlab then also invoked her right to FoRB under Article 9 of the European Convention on Human Rights, countering that refusing to allow her to wear the headscarf was a violation of this right. As with *Lautsi*, the *Dahlab* case was first heard within the national legal system, in this case Swiss, before being heard by the ECtHR in 2001.

The ruling in the *Dahlab* case touched on the exact same issues with regard to the headscarf as the Grand Chamber *Lautsi* ruling also would in relation to the crucifix a decade later. The Court found that the headscarf is a "powerful religious symbol" which does violate the principle of neutrality in the classroom. They further determined that the headscarf has "some kind of proselytizing effect", influencing "the freedom of conscience of very young children", despite the fact that Ms Dahlab never discussed her religious commitments with her

## 118  *Religion in Human Rights, Law, and Public Life*

students. In addition, the Court stated that the headscarf is "imposed on women by ... the Koran" and undermines tolerance, equality, respect for others, non-discrimination, and democracy (Dahlab v Switzerland 2001). In both cases, the ECtHR makes explicit pronouncements regarding the meaning of both symbols, an act that could be viewed as theological and a precarious move for a nominally secular institution that should be neutral when it comes to matters of religion.

The difference between the two rulings is striking, visualised in Table 5.1.

The outcome in both cases was most likely shaped by the so-called *margin of appreciation* rule, in which European Union member states are ultimately allowed self-determination when it comes to the implementation of law and the realisation of human rights. In cases such as *Dahlab* and *Lautsi*, the ECtHR will therefore often find in favour of the state party to the case (Beaman 2013). Not only is the regulation of religious symbols in public life a site of power contestation between majority and minority religions, it is also a site of contestation between individuals and the power of the state.

A similarly contradictory legal situation arose in the German state of Bavaria in 2018. In March of that year, a Muslim legal trainee was denied the right to wear a headscarf in court. The judge's ruling in the case again cited the importance of "independence and neutrality" of the courtroom (Pearson 2018). Yet in May of the same year, the

*Table 5.1* Comparison of *Dahlab v Switzerland* and *Lautsi and others v Italy*

| *Dahlab v Switzerland (2001)* | *Lautsi and others v Italy (2011)* |
| --- | --- |
| The headscarf: | The crucifix: |
| a "*powerful* religious symbol*", violating the principle of neutrality | "*an essentially _passive_ symbol*", does not violate the principle of neutrality |
| Has "*some kind of _proselytizing effect_*", influencing "*the freedom of conscience of very young children*" | "*No evidence ... that the display of a religious symbol on classroom walls _may have an influence on pupils_*" |
| Is "*imposed on women by ... the Koran*" and undermines tolerance, equality, respect for others, non-discrimination, and democracy | Is a religious but also cultural symbol, part of Italian cultural heritage, evoking principles of democracy, equality, non-violence, justice |

Sources: Evans (2006), European Court of Human Rights Grand Chamber (2011).

*Religion in Human Rights, Law, and Public Life* 119

government of Bavaria introduced a law requiring that all state authorities in Bavaria have a cross hanging in their foyer "to serve as a reminder of the historical and cultural influence of Bavaria" (Staudenmaier 2018). Yet again, the distinction between "religion" and "culture" is politically salient.

These efforts to police religious symbols in the public sphere have intensified as concerns about Islam in Europe have grown, with Muslim women and the wearing of headscarves the primary target of these different legal initiatives. Gender inequality and religious discrimination intersect in these controversies, with women's bodies becoming the site through which contestations of political and cultural identity take place (as can also be observed in the deeply controversial overturning of *Roe v Wade* by the US Supreme Court in June 2022). The headscarf, so the argument goes, is a symbol of women's oppression. It is antithetical to the values of secularism that include gender equality and emancipation. Within this framework, religion is constructed as traditional, conservative, and patriarchal, while secularism is modern, progressive, and emancipatory. Yet as we explored in Chapter 4, there are multifarious positions amongst actors who identify as "religious" and "secular" on issues of gender equality, women's rights, and emancipation. Further, the agency of religious women in such debates and legal rulings is completely ignored. The underlying assumption is that women are forced to wear the headscarf, or other face or body covering, and must therefore be liberated or rescued from their oppression (Abu-Lughod 2002). In France during the burkini saga of 2016, women were issued with fines for not wearing an "outfit respecting good morals and secularism" (Quinn 2016), while then French Prime Minister Manuel Valls claimed that naked breasts were more representative of French freedom and values than a headscarf (Chrisafis 2016). Conversely, because of the increasing securitisation of Islam and the veil in Europe and European-influenced contexts, if women do choose to veil, then they represent extremist Islamist views which must be restricted (Edmunds 2021). Little to no credence is given to the possibility that women may choose to veil or un-/de-veil in line with how they wish to manifest and observe their religion (Scott 2007; Fadil 2011). Further, as Joan Scott (2007) argues, *laique* and secular efforts forcing Muslim women to "de-veil" because the veil is seen as a symbol of women's oppression are just as oppressive and discriminatory as the practice of forced veiling itself. In such narratives, women, whether they identify as Muslim or otherwise, become objects within public politics onto which those in power (often, though not always, men) write their own narratives and agendas concerning religion in the public sphere.

## Conclusion

The diverse examples explored in this chapter demonstrate that the meaning and interpretation of "religion" with respect to law and human rights is rarely consistent. Rather, individual legal and political authorities apply their own definitions and understandings of what "religion" is, informed by the broader social, cultural, and political debates taking place at the time, to decide the outcomes of these cases. The consequences of such rulings can result in increasing marginalisation for minorities, heightened feelings and experiences of insecurity, discrimination, detrimental impacts on health and well-being, and the denial of fundamental rights and freedoms. They can also have consequences for international diplomacy and advocacy. In the contemporary transnational environment, ideas about "religion", "law", and "human rights" migrate across different legal and socio-political contexts, making domestic developments pertinent to international law and human rights. The observable difference between approaches to the right to FoRB in domestic European legislation and the support for FoRB increasingly expressed in European foreign policy highlights an emerging double standard that has the potential to impede international efforts to promote and protect the right to FoRB. Law is not neutral, but a codification and reflection of the broader values and cultural norms informing the structure of society (Berger 2018). It is shaped by historical legacies of colonial encounters, differing and often contradictory assumptions about the meaning of key terms and phrases, such as "religion" or "religious freedom", inequalities and power imbalances between minority and majority communities, and between individuals and the state. Making sense of religions' relationship with law and human rights thus requires application of insights from critical and intersectional theory, a nuanced consideration of context, and a precise articulation of what we mean by "religion" in specific cases and examples.

## Note

1 https://aiatsis.gov.au/explore/living-languages.

# Conclusion

The study of religion in IR has for too long been governed by preconceived secularist understandings of the category of religion. Critical scholars have deprived this dominant paradigm of its hegemony in recent decades, highlighting the multifarious problematic and damaging assumptions guiding attitudes towards religion in international diplomacy, law, security, foreign policy, development, and humanitarianism. What has been missing, however, is a clear and practical guide for scholars, policymakers, and practitioners for how to analyse and approach religion differently, in a more holistic and contextually embedded way.

This book has offered one such guide: a critical, intersectional analytical framework that rests on three principles. First, analysis of religion and IR needs to depart not from an abstract and often ill-defined concept of "religion", but instead begin by engaging with specific issues or contexts and explore what "religion" means in those situations. Second, "religion" should not be analysed in isolation but must be considered in connection with other socio-political factors. Third, rather than referring to an undifferentiated idea of "religion", we need to break this category down and focus on the actors, narratives, and identities as well as specific religious traditions that are relevant within the parameters of the context or issue we are analysing. In other words, this framework privileges a focus on lived religion: how religion is understood, engaged with, and practised by individuals and communities within specific contexts and how this shapes and is shaped by different policies and events within world politics. Such a focus is essential because "religion" does not mean the same thing at all times and in all places. Through the various case studies explored throughout the book, I have demonstrated that what "religion" means is highly dependent on the situation, the issue, the actors, and the power relations involved. Departing from a focus on context first,

DOI: 10.4324/9781003037057-6

## 122   *Conclusion*

rather than on "religion", enables a fuller appreciation of these different dynamics, reducing the possibilities for miscalculations, mistakes, and missteps that can and have had dire consequences for individuals and communities around the world.

An appreciation of lived religion is invaluable for IR analysis because it reminds us of the real experienced consequences for individuals and communities. The study of IR in general, and of religion in particular, is often disconnected from the lived realities of individuals and communities, owing to the predominant focus of IR on states and the states-system. Yet states, after all, are established, governed, made up of, and lived in by people. Studying the place of religion within international politics without reference to the lived realities of individuals and communities risks overlooking or ignoring the very real implications for people that come from the decisions taken by those working in diplomacy, security, development, law, and human rights.

This means that adopting critical approaches to the study of religion and world politics is not only relevant for academics. Definitions of religion are not purely abstract, theoretical, or conceptual, nor are they only relevant for academics as my Oxford coffee companion asserted. As the cases throughout the book demonstrate, the way analysts, policymakers, development practitioners, lawyers, and human rights activists understand religion and apply this understanding in their work has real, sometimes life and death, consequences for individuals and communities all over the world. How we define religion matters and that is why we have to be so careful, meticulous, and precise when we do it. This is not to suggest that we must develop a stable, universal conceptualisation of religion that can be deployed in our analysis. Such an endeavour would inevitably end up privileging one specific historical, socio-political, cultural understanding and experience of what religion is (which is precisely what has occurred with the dominance of secularisms in IR and the modern state and states-system: the privileging of Euro-American conceptions of "religion", informed by experiences of Christianity). Rather, we must acknowledge and work with the diversity and instability of this concept, in a way that enriches and informs our research, analysis, policymaking, and practice, through privileging the perspectives and experiences of the people living in the specific contexts that we are investigating.

In developing this hopefully practical guide for how to study religion and IR from a critical intersectional perspective, this book has also tried to demonstrate that critical approaches are not just the preserve of academia. Being "critical" is not just about highlighting what is problematic in the existing ways that we approach particular

*Conclusion* 123

subjects, such as religion, although it is a necessary and imperative first step. Being "critical" is about understanding where problematic assumptions come from and identifying possibilities for addressing and changing those assumptions. Being "critical" is about acknowledging multiple perspectives, informed by particular historical, political, geographic, cultural, and discursive contexts and learning from and incorporating those diverse perspectives in our scholarship and our political practices. Acknowledging these different perspectives is essential for all of us, within and outside academia. It enables us to better understand the world around us, and develop research, policies, and civil society projects and programmes that more accurately and effectively respond to the world as it is, not merely as we think it is or as we think it should be.

On a day-to-day basis in policymaking and practice, incorporating critical perspectives on religion in IR includes some of the following steps:

- Ensure that policy and project initiatives reflect no normative position regarding whether religion is "positive" or "negative". It is a socio-political phenomenon to be analysed, understood, and engaged with as part of whole-of-society approaches.
- Go beyond the "usual suspects" when working with religious actors, reaching out especially to marginalised groups (particularly women, LGBTQI+, and young people), recognising that established religious authorities and leaders are not the only or even the most relevant actors in specific contexts on particular issues. Work with these actors in ways that do not put already marginalised groups at further risk.
- Deliberately incorporate attention for and knowledge of religious traditions beyond Christianity and Islam in policymaking and practice.
- Be aware that labels such as "religious" and "secular" do not always resonate outside Euro-American contexts. Even within Europe and North America, the meanings of these labels are not necessarily shared or consistent.
- Acknowledge historical inequalities and power imbalances that continue to affect international political relationships.
- Avoid centralising or marginalising religion in analysis of international security, development, humanitarianism, and human rights issues. Pay attention to religious dynamics, but in a balanced way that acknowledges their connections with other factors such as class, race, gender, sexuality, and ethnicity.

## 124   *Conclusion*

- Remember that religious actors are diverse, heterogeneous, and represent a vast array of perspectives on socio-political issues, from conservative and traditional to radical and progressive.
- Bear in mind that religious actors carry more influence and legitimacy in some contexts than government or state authorities.

This book represents one way of practically incorporating insights from critical intersectional scholarship into our analysis and policymaking on religion and IR. There are undoubtedly a multitude of others, and I look forward to this one being surpassed by other more sophisticated, more nuanced, more practical approaches in the future.

# Bibliography

Abdul-Hamid, Walid Khalid and Jamie Hacker Hughes. 2015. "Integration of Religion and Spirituality into Trauma and Psychotherapy: An Example in Sufism?" *Journal of EMDR Practice and Research* 9, no. 3: 150–156.

Abrams, Abigail. 2015. "Paris Attack 2015: Named Terrorists All European Nationals, Not Syrian Refugees." *International Business Times.* November 19, 2015. Accessed on June 27, 2022. https://www.ibtimes.com/paris-attack-2015-named-terrorists-all-european-nationals-not-syrian-refugees-2191677.

Abu-Lughod, Lila. 2002. "Do Muslim Women Really Need Saving? Anthropological Reflections on Cultural Relativism and Its Other." *American Anthropologist* 104, no. 3: 783–790.

Adami, Rebecca. 2012. "Reconciling Universality and Particularity through a Cosmopolitan Outlook on Human Rights." *Cosmopolitan Civil Societies Journal* 4, no. 2: 22–37.

Ager, Alastair and Joey Ager. 2011. "Faith and the Discourse of Secular Humanitarianism." *Journal of Refugee Studies* 24, no. 3: 456–472.

Ager, Joey, Behailu Abebe and Alastair Ager. 2014. "Mental Health and Psychosocial Support in Humanitarian Emergencies in Africa: Challenges and Opportunities for Engaging with the Faith Sector." *Review of Faith and International Affairs* 12, no. 1: 72–83.

Ager, Wendy, Michael French, Atallah Fitzgibbon and Alastair Ager. 2019. "The Case for – and Challenges of – Faith-Sensitive Psychosocial Programming." *Interventions* 17, no. 1: 69–75.

Akins, Harrison. 2018. "The Two Faces of Democratization in Myanmar: A Case Study of the Rohingya and Burmese Nationalism." *Journal of Muslim Minority Affairs* 38, no. 2: 229–245.

Al-Marashi, Ibrahim. 2021. "Demobilization Minus Disarmament and Reintegration: Iraq's Security Sector from the US Occupation to the COVID19 Pandemic." *Journal of Intervention and Statebuilding* 15, no. 4: 441–458.

Alshamary, Marsin Rahim. 2021. "Religious Peacebuilding in Iraq: Prospects and Challenges from the Hawza." *Journal of Intervention and Statebuilding* 15, no. 4: 494–509.

## 126  *Bibliography*

Amanpour, Christiane and Thom Patterson. 2015. "Passport Linked to Terrorist Complicate Syrian Refugee Crisis." *CNN*. November 15, 2015. Accessed on June 27, 2022. https://edition.cnn.com/2015/11/15/europe/paris-attacks-passports/.

Arifin, Syamsul. 2012. "Indonesian Discourse on Human Rights and Freedom of Religion or Belief: Muslim Perspectives." *BYU Law Review* 2012, no. 3: 775–808.

Arraf, Jane. 2021. "U.S. Announces End to Combat Mission in Iraq, But Troops Will Not Leave." *The New York Times*. December 9, 2021. Accessed on April 11, 2022. https://www.nytimes.com/2021/12/09/world/middleeast/us-iraq-combat-mission.html.

Asad, Talal. 2003. *Formations of the Secular: Christianity, Islam, Modernity*. Stanford, CA: Stanford University Press.

Asch, Ronald Gregor. 1997. *The Thirty Years' War: The Holy Roman Empire and Europe 1618–1648*. New York: St Martin's Press.

Auger, Vincent. 2020. "Right-Wing Terror: A Fifth Global Wave?" *Perspectives on Terrorism* 14, no. 3: 87–97.

Bakali, Naved and Shujaat Wasty. 2020. "Identity, Social Mobility, and Trauma: Post-Conflict Educational Realities for Survivors of the Rohingya Genocide." *Religions* 11: 241–255.

Barnett, Michael and Janice Gross Stein. 2012. *Sacred Aid: Faith and Humanitarianism*. New York: Oxford University Press.

Barrère, Jean-Bertrand. 2022. "Victor Hugo." *Encyclopedia Britannica*. Accessed on June 20, 2022. https://www.britannica.com/biography/Victor-Hugo.

Bartelink, Brenda Elizabeth. 2021. "Gender and International Development: Searching for Game Changers in the Midst of Polarization." In *The Routledge Handbook of Religion, Gender and Society*, edited by Caroline Starkey and Emma Tomalin, 351–364. London: Routledge.

Bartelink, Brenda Elizabeth and Elisabet Le Roux. 2018. "Navigating State, Religion and Gender: A Case Study of ABAAD's Gender Activism in Lebanon." *Politeia* 37, no. 2: 1–22. https://doi.org/10.25159/0256-8845/4653.

Bartelink, Brenda Elizabeth and Erin Kate Wilson. 2020. "The Spiritual Is Political: Reflecting on Gender, Religion and Secularism in International Development." In *International Development and Local Faith Actors*, edited by Kathryn Kraft and Olivia Wilkinson, 45–58. London: Routledge.

BBC. 2021. "Oxfam: UK Halts Funding after New Sexual Exploitation Claims." *BBC News*. April 7, 2021. Accessed on June 30, 2022. https://www.bbc.com/news/health-56670162.

BBC. 2021. "US Combat Forces to Leave Iraq by End of Year." Accessed on July 27, 2021. https://www.bbc.com/news/world-us-canada-57970464.

Beaman, Lori. 2013. "Battle over Symbols: The "Religion" of the Minority and the "Culture" of the Majority." *Journal of Law and Religion* 28, no. 1: 67–104.

Beaman, Lori., Jennifer Selby and Amélie Barras. 2016. "No Mosque, No Refuges: Some Reflections on Syrian Refugees and the Construction of

## Bibliography 127

Religion in Canada." In *The Refugee Crisis and Religion: Secularism, Security and Hospitality in Question*, edited by Luca Mavelli and Erin Kate Wilson, 77–96. London: Rowman and Littlefield International.

Becci, Irene, Marian Burchardt and Mariachiara Giorda. 2016. "Religious Super-Diversity and Spatial Strategies in Two European Cities." *Current Sociology* 65, no. 1: 73–91.

Bell, Derek. 2013. "Climate Change and Human Rights." *WIREs Climate Change* 4, no. 3: 159–170.

Bellah, Robert. 2005. "Civil Religion in America." *Daedalus* 134, no. 4: 40–55.

Berger, Benjamin. 2018. *Law's Religion: Religious Difference and the Claims of Constitutionalism*. Toronto: University of Toronto Press.

Berger, Peter, Marjo Buitelaar and Kim Knibbe. 2021. "Introduction: Religion as Relation." In *Religion as Relation: Studying Religion in Context*, edited by Peter Berger, Marjo Buitelaar and Kim KnibbeSheffield: Equinox.

Bertana, Amanda. 2021. "Religious Explanations for Coastal Erosion in Narikoso, Fiji." In *Understanding Climate Change through Religious Lifeworlds*, edited by David L. Haberman, 77–97. Bloomington, IN: Indiana University Press.

Blackbourn, Jessie, Nicola McGarrity and Kent Roach. 2019. "Understanding and Responding to Right-Wing Terrorism." *Journal of Policing, Intelligence and Counter-Terrorism* 14, no. 3: 183–190.

Blaser, Mario. 2013. "Ontological Conflicts and Stories of Peoples in Spite of Europe." *Current Anthropology* 54, no. 5: 547–568.

Brown, Katherine. 2020. "Religious Violence, Gender and Post-secular Counterterrorism." *International Affairs* 96, no. 2: 279–303.

Brzozowski, Wojciech. 2021. "Did Pastafarians Lose in Strasbourg, After All?" *Oxford Journal of Law and Religion* 10, no. 3: 487–494.

Buijs, Frank. 2009. "Muslims in the Netherlands: Social and Political Developments after 9/11." *Journal of Ethnic and Migration Studies* 35, no. 3: 421–438.

Bullock, Katherine. 2022. "Ukraine War Shows It's Time to Do Away with the Racist 'Clash of Civilizations' Theory." *The Conversation*. March 21, 2022. Accessed on June 21, 2022. https://theconversation.com/ukraine-war-shows-its-time-to-do-away-with-the-racist-clash-of-civilizations-theory-178297.

Campbell, David. 1998. *Writing Security: United States Foreign Policy and the Politics of Identity*. Manchester: Manchester University Press.

Casanova, José. 2011. "The Secular, Secularizations, Secularisms." In *Rethinking Secularism*, edited by Craig Calhoun, Mark Juergensmeyer and Jonathan van Antwerpen, 54–74. Oxford: Oxford University Press.

Castelli, Elisabeth. 2007. "Theologizing Human Rights: Christian Activism and the Limits of Religious Freedom." In *Nongovernmental Politics*, edited by Michael Feher, Yates McKee and Gaëlle Krikorian, 673–687. New York: Zone Books.

Cavanaugh, William. 2009. *The Myth of Religious Violence*. Oxford: Oxford University Press.

Charney, Michael. 2021. "Myanmar Coup: How the Military has Held on to Power for 60 Years." *The Conversation*. February 3, 2021. Accessed on July 26,

## 128  Bibliography

2021.https://theconversation.com/myanmar-coup-how-the-military-has-held-onto-power-for-60-years-154526.

Cherry, Conrad. 1998. *God's New Israel: Religious Interpretations of America's Destiny*. Chapel Hill, NC: University of North Carolina Press.

Chowdhury Fink, Naureen and Rafia Bhulai. 2016. "Development and Countering Violent Extremism." *Sustainable Development Goals 2016*. Accessed on December 14, 2021. https://www.sustainablegoals.org.uk/wp-content/uploads/2016/03/048-051_CHOWDHURY-Meeting-the-demand_OL.pdf.

Chrisafis, Angelique. 2016. "French PM Suggests Naked Breasts Represent France Better than a Headscarf." *The Guardian*. August 30, 2016. Accessed on June 12, 2022. https://www.theguardian.com/world/2016/aug/30/france-manuel-valls-breasts-headscarf-burkini-ban-row.

Church of the Flying Spaghetti Monster. "About." Last modified in 2022. Accessed on May 23, 2022. https://www.spaghettimonster.org/about/.

Clarke, Gerard. 2006. "Faith Matters: Faith-Based Organisations, Civil Society and International Development." *Journal of International Development* 18, no. 6: 835–848.

Conway, Janet. 2013. *Edges of Global Justice: The World Social Forum and Its Others*. Lanham, MD: Rowman and Littlefield.

Cuddy, Alice. 2021. "Myanmar Coup: What Is Happening and Why?" *BBC News*. April 1, 2021. Accessed on July 27, 2021. https://www.bbc.com/news/world-asia-55902070.

Daulatzai, Anila. 2004. "A Leap of Faith: Thoughts on Secularistic Practices and Progressive Politics." *International Social Science Journal* 56, no. 182: 565–576.

Deneulin, Séverine. 2021. "Religion and Development: Integral Ecology and the Catholic Church Amazon Synod." *Third World Quarterly* 42, no. 10: 2282–2299.

Donnelly, Jack. 2013. *Universal Human Rights in Theory and Practice*. Ithaca, NY: Cornell University Press.

Doosje, Bertjan, Fathali Moghaddam, Arie Kruglanski, Arjan de Wolf, Liesbeth Mann and Allard Feddes. 2016. "Terrorism, Radicalization and De-radicalization." *Current Opinion in Psychology* 11: 79–84.

Douthat, Ross. 2022. "Yes, There Is a Clash of Civilizations." *The New York Times*. March 30, 2022. Accessed on June 21, 2022. https://www.nytimes.com/2022/03/30/opinion/ukraine-clash-of-civilizations.html.

Duile, Timo. 2018. "Atheism in Indonesia: State Discourses of the Past and Social Practices of the Present." *South East Asia Research* 26, no. 2: 161–175.

Dzuhayatin, Siti Ruhaini. 2015. "Gender as a Social Regime in the Islamic Context – the Case of the Muhammidiya." In *Indonesian and German Views on the Islamic Legal Discourse on Gender and Civil Rights*, edited by Noorhaidi Hasan and Fritze Schultze, 45–60. Wiesbaden, Gottingen: Harrassowitz Verslag.

Edkins, Jenny. 2019. "Introduction." In *Routledge Handbook of Critical International Relations*, edited by Jenny Edkins, 1–8. London: Routledge.

Edmunds, Aneira. 2021. "Precarious Bodies: The Securitization of the "Veiled" Woman in European Human Rights." *British Journal of Sociology* 72, no. 2: 315–327.

## Bibliography 129

Eghdamian, Khatereh. 2016. "Religious Identity and Experiences of Displacement: An Examination into the Discursive Representations of Syrian Refugees and Their Effects on Religious Minorities Living in Jordan." *Journal of Refugee Studies* 30, no. 3: 447–467.

Esposito, John. 2019. "Islamophobia and Radicalization: Roots, Impact and Implications." In *Islamophobia and Radicalization*, edited by John Esposito and Derya Iner, 15–33 Cham: Palgrave Macmillan.

Esposito, John and Derya Iner (eds). 2018. *Islamophobia and Radicalization: Breeding Intolerance and Violence*. Cham: Springer International.

European Court of Human Rights Grand Chamber. 2011. "Case of Lautsi and Others v Italy Judgement." March 18, 2011. Accessed on July 6, 2018. http://hudoc.echr.coe.int/app/conversion/pdf/?library=ECHR&id=001-104040&filename=001-104040.pdf.

European Union. 2021. *Contemporary Manifestations of Violent Right-Wing Extremism in the EU: An Overview of PICVE Practices*. Luxembourg: Publication Office of the European Union. Accessed on November 17, 2021. https://ec.europa.eu/home-affairs/system/files/2021-04/ran_adhoc_cont_manif_vrwe_eu_overv_pcve_pract_2021_en.pdf.

Evans, Carolyn. 2006. "The "Islamic Scarf" in the European Court of Human Rights" *Melbourne Journal of International Law* 7, no. 1. Accessed on January 9, 2018. http://classic.austlii.edu.au/au/journals/MelbJIL/2006/4.html.

Fadil, Nadia. 2011. "Not-/Unveiling as an Ethical Practice." *Feminist Review* 98: 83–109.

Fiddian-Qasmiyeh, Elena. 2014. *The Ideal Refugees: Gender, Islam, and the Sahrawi Politics of Survival*. New York: Syracuse University Press.

Fiddian-Qasmiyeh, Elena. 2016. "The Faith-Gender-Asylum Nexus: An Intersectionalist Analysis of Representations of the 'Refugee Crisis'." In *The Refugee Crisis and Religion: Secularism, Security and Hospitality in Question*, edited by Luca Mavelli and Erin Kate Wilson, 207–222. London: Rowman and Littlefield International.

Forsythe, David. 2000. *Human Rights in International Relations*. Cambridge: Cambridge University Press.

Fowler, Corinne. 2007. *Chasing Tales: Travel Writing, Journalism and the History of British Ideas about Afghanistan*. Amsterdam: Rodopi.

Foxeus, Niklas. 2019. "The Buddha was a Devoted Nationalist: Buddhist nationalism, *Ressentiment* and Defending Buddhism in Myanmar." *Religion* 49, no. 4: 661–690.

Freeman, Michael. 2004. "The Problem of Secularism in Human Rights Theory." *Human Rights Quarterly* 26, no. 2: 375–400.

Freeman, Michael. 2017. *Human Rights: An Interdisciplinary Approach*. 3rd ed. London: Polity Press.

Frydenlund, Iselin, Pum Za Mang, Phyo Wai and Susan Hayward. 2021. "Religious Responses to the Military Coup in Myanmar." *The Review of Faith & International Affairs* 19, no. 3: 77–88. https://doi.org/10.1080/15570274.2021.1954409.

Galtung, Johan. 1969. "Violence, Peace, and Peace Research." *Journal of Peace Research* 6, no. 3: 167–191.

## 130  Bibliography

Galtung, Johan. 1996. *Peace by Peaceful Means: Peace and Conflict, Development and Civilization*. London: Sage Publications.

Gozdziak, Elzbieta. 2002. "Spiritual Emergency Room: The Role of Spirituality and Religion in the Resettlement of Kosovar Albanians." *Journal of Refugee Studies* 15, no. 2: 136–152.

Grim, Brian and Roger Finke. 2011. *The Price of Freedom Denied: Religious Persecution and Conflict in the Twenty-First Century*. Cambridge: Cambridge University Press.

Grüll, Christoph and Erin Kate Wilson. 2018. "Universal or Particular or Both? Understanding the Right to Freedom of Religion or Belief in Cross-Cultural Perspective." *Review of Faith and International Affairs* 16, no. 4: 88–101.

Guerrera, Dominic. 2021. "We Don't Fabricate, We Weave: Kumarangk (Hindmarsh Island) and Ngarrindjeri Women's Resistance." *Artlink*. December 15, 2021. Accessed on June 12, 2022. https://www.artlink.com.au/articles/4950/we-donE28099t-fabricate-we-weave-kumarangk-28hindmarsh-i/.

Guterres, António. 2019. "Remarks at 2019 Climate Action Summit." *United Nations*. September 23, 2019. Accessed on April 19, 2022. https://www.un.org/sg/en/content/sg/speeches/2019-09-23/remarks-2019-climate-action-summit.

Guterres, António. 2021. "Deputy Secretary-General's Video Message to the G20 Interfaith Forum." *United Nations*. September 12, 2021. Accessed on April 19, 2022. https://www.un.org/sg/en/content/dsg/statement/2021-09-12/deputy-secretary-generals-video-message-the-g20-interfaith-forum.

Gutkowski, Stacey. 2011. "Secularism and the Politics of Risk: Britain's Prevent Agenda, 2005–2009." *International Relations* 25, no. 3: 346–362.

Gutkowski, Stacey. 2014. *Secular War: Myths of Religion, Politics and Violence*. London and New York: I.B. Tauris.

de Haan, Sanneke. 2017. "The Existential Dimension in Psychiatry: An Enactive Framework." *Mental Health, Religion and Culture* 20, no. 6: 528–535.

Hafez, Farid, Reinhard Heinisch and Eric Miklin. 2019. "The New Right: Austria's Freedom Party and Changing Perceptions of Islam." *The Brookings Institute*. Accessed on November 17, 2021. https://www.brookings.edu/research/the-new-right-austrias-freedom-party-and-changing-perceptions-of-islam/.

Harper, Mary. 2019. *Everything You Have Told Me Is True: The Many Faces of Al-Shabaab*. London: Hurst and Company.

Hayward, Susan and Iselin Frydenlund. 2019. "Religion, Secularism, and the Pursuit of Peace in Myanmar." *The Review of Faith & International Affairs* 17, no. 4: 1–11.

Helfont, Samuel. 2018. *Compulsion in Religion: Saddam Hussein, Islam, and the Roots of Insurgencies in Iraq*. New York: Oxford University Press.

Henne, Peter, Sarabrynn Hudgins and Timothy Samuel Shah. 2012. *Religious Freedom and Violent Religious Extremism: A Sourcebook of Modern Cases and Analysis*. Washington, DC: Berkeley Center for Religion, Peace, and World Affairs, Georgetown University.

Hertzke, Allen. 2012. "Introduction." In *The Future of Religious Freedom*, edited by Allen. Hertzke, 3–27. Oxford: Oxford University Press.

## Bibliography 131

Hoffarth, Mark Romeo and Gordon Hodson. 2016. "Green on the Outside, Red on the Inside: Perceived Environmentalist Threat as a Factor Explaining Political Polarization of Climate Change." *Journal of Environmental Psychology* 45: 40–49.

Hopgood, Stephen and Leslie Vinjamuri. 2012. "Faith in Markets." In *Sacred Aid: Faith and Humanitarianism*, edited by Michael Barnet and Janice Gross Stein, 37–64. Oxford: Oxford University Press.

Hoskins, Janet. 2007. "Caodai Exile and Redemption: A New Vietnamese Religion's Struggle for Identity." In *Religion and Social Justice for Immigrants*, edited by Pierette Hondagneu-Sotelo, 191–209. New Brunswick, NJ: Rutgers.

Hoskins, Janet. 2015. *The Divine Eye and the Diaspora: Vietnamese Syncretism Becomes Transpacific Caodaism*. Honolulu: University of Hawai'i Press.

Houston, Aidan and Peter Mandaville. 2022. "The Role of Religion in Russia's War on Ukraine." *United States Institute of Peace*. Accessed on June 23, 2022. https://www.usip.org/publications/2022/03/role-religion-russias-war-ukraine.

Hulme, Mike. 2017. "Climate Change and the Significance of Religion." *Economic and Political Weekly* 52, no. 28: 14–17.

Huntington, Samuel. 1993. "The Clash of Civilizations?" *Foreign Affairs* 72, no. 3: 22–50.

Hurd, Elizabeth Shakman. 2008. *The Politics of Secularism in International Relations*. Princeton, NJ: Princeton University Press.

Hurd, Elizabeth Shakman. 2015. *Beyond Religious Freedom: The New Global Politics of Religion*. Princeton, NJ: Princeton University Press.

Ishay, Micheline. 2008. *The History of Human Rights: From Ancient Times to the Era of Globalization*. Berkeley, CA: University of California Press.

Johnson, Sarah. 2022. "Racism in Aid Sector Is a Hangover of Colonialism, Says Scathing Report by MPs." *The Guardian*. June 23, 2022. Accessed on June 24, 2022. https://www.theguardian.com/global-development/2022/jun/23/racism-in-aid-sector-is-a-hangover-of-colonialism-says-scathing-report-by-mps.

Jones, Ben and Marie Juul Petersen. 2011. "Instrumental, Narrow, Normative? Reviewing Recent Work on Religion and Development." *Third World Quarterly* 32, no. 7: 1291–1306.

Jones, David Martin and M. L. R. Smith (Michael Rainsbourgh). 2005. "Greetings from the Cybercaliphate: Some Notes on Homeland Insecurity." *International Affairs* 81, no. 5: 925–950.

Kalenychenko, Tatiana and Denys Brylov. 2022. "Ukrainian Religious Actors and Organizations After Russia's Invasion: The Struggle For Peace." *Transatlantic Policy Network for Religion and Diplomacy*. Available at https://religionanddiplomacy.org/wp-content/uploads/2022/09/220913KalenychenkoBrylovUkrainianReligiousActorsAfterRussianInvasionPolicyBrief.pdf Accessed 26 October 2022

Kam, Stefanie and Michael Clarke. 2021. "Securitization, Surveillance and 'De-extremization' in Xinjiang." *International Affairs* 97, no. 3: 625–642.

Karam, Azza. 2012. "Religion, Development and the United Nations" *Social Science Research Council Report*. New York: Social Science Research

## 132 *Bibliography*

Council. Accessed April 18, 2022 https://www.ssrc.org/publications/religion-development-and-the-united-nations/

Kartinyeri, Doreen and Sue Anderson. 2008. *My Ngarrindjeri Calling.* Canberra: Aboriginal Studies Press.

Keane, Daniel. 2021. "Church of the Flying Spaghetti Monster Loses Bid for Legal Recognition as Incorporated Entity." *ABC News.* June 19, 2021. Accessed on May 23, 2022. https://www.abc.net.au/news/2021-06-19/sa-church-of-the-flying-spaghetti-monster-proposal-rejected/100228038.

Kelly, Robert. 2022. "Is the War in Ukraine a Clash of Civilizations? Not Exactly." *1945.* April 5, 2022. Accessed on June 22, 2022. https://www.19fortyfive.com/2022/04/is-the-war-in-ukraine-a-clash-of-civilizations-not-exactly/.

Keyzer, Patrick. 2020. "Section 71: The Hindmarsh Island Bridge Affairs, Parts One and Two." *The History Listen with Kristi Melville* [Podcast]. Broadcast dates: May 26 and June 2, 2020. Accessed on June 12, 2022. https://www.abc.net.au/radionational/programs/the-history-listen/section-71:-the-hindmarsh-island-bridge-affair-(part-1)/12202724.

Kidwai, Sadia. 2016. "The Limits of Hospitality: Finding Space for Faith." In *The Refugee Crisis and Religion: Secularism, Security and Hospitality in Question*, edited by L. Mavelli and E. K. Wilson, 175–186. London: Rowman and Littlefield International.

Ki-moon, Ban. 2008. "Faith Communities Have a Crucial Role to Play in Fostering Mutual Understanding and in Promoting Consensus on Common Values and Aspirations." *United Nations Information Service (UNIS) Vienna.* July 16, 2008. Accessed on April 19, 2022. https://unis.unvienna.org/unis/pressrels/2008/unissgsm058.html.

Ki-moon, Ban. 2009. "Secretary-General's speech to Summit of Religious and Secular Leaders on Climate Change [as prepared for delivery]." *United Nations.* November 3, 2009. Accessed on April 19, 2022. https://www.un.org/sg/en/content/sg/statement/2009-11-03/secretary-generals-speech-summit-religious-and-secular-leaders.

Kirmanj, Şêrko. 2013. *Identity and Nation in Iraq.* Boulder, CO: Lynne Rienner Publishers.

Kissinger, Henry. 2014. "To Settle the Ukraine Crisis, Start at the End." *The Washington Post.* March 5, 2014. Accessed on June 20, 2022. https://www.washingtonpost.com/opinions/henry-kissinger-to-settle-the-ukraine-crisis-start-at-the-end/2014/03/05/46dad868-a496-11e3-8466-d34c451760b9_story.html.

Klöck, Carola. 2015. "Adapting to Climate Change in Small Island Developing States." *Climate Change* 133, no. 3: 481–489.

Knaus, Christopher and Michael McGowan. 2021. "Who's Behind Australia's Anti-Lockdown Protests? The German Conspiracy Group Driving Marches." *The Guardian.* July 27, 2021. Accessed on April 12, 2022. https://www.theguardian.com/australia-news/2021/jul/27/who-behind-australia-anti-covid-lockdown-protest-march-rallies-sydney-melbourne-far-right-and-german-conspiracy-groups-driving-protests.

## Bibliography 133

Koehler, Daniel. 2016. *Right-Wing Terrorism in the 21st Century: The 'National Socialist Underground' and the History of Terror from the Far-Right in Germany.* London: Routledge.

Koslander, Tiburtius, António Barbosa da Silva and Asa Roxberg. 2009. "Existential and Spiritual Needs in Mental Health Care: An Ethical and Holistic Perspective." *Journal of Holistic Nursing* 27, no. 1: 34–42.

Kozelsky, Mara. 2014. "Religion and the Crisis in Ukraine." *International Journal for the Study of the Christian Church* 14, no. 3: 219–241.

Kristimanta, Putri Ariza. 2021. "Grass-Roots Post-conflict Peacebuilding: A Case Study of Mosintuwu Women's School in Poso District, Central Sulawesi, Indonesia." In *Decolonising Conflicts, Security, Peace, Gender, Environment and Development in the Anthropocene*, edited by Úrsula Oswald and Hans Günter Brauch, 569–590. Cham: Springer.

Kubalkova, Vendulka. 2013. "The "Turn to Religion" in International Relations Theory." *E-International Relations.* December 3, 2013. Accessed on March 29, 2021. https://www.e-ir.info/2013/12/03/the-turn-to-religion-in-international-relations-theory/.

Kuru, Ahmed. 2009. *Secularism and State Policies towards Religion.* Cambridge: Cambridge University Press.

Laksana, Ben and Barbara Wood. 2019. "Navigating Religious Diversity: Exploring Young People's Lived Religious Citizenship in Indonesia." *Journal of Youth Studies* 22, no. 6: 807–823.

Langton, Marcia. 1996. "The Hindmarsh Island Bridge Affair: How Aboriginal Women's Religion Became an Administerable Affair." *Australian Feminist Studies* 11, no. 24: 211–217.

Lata, Shanini and Patrick Nunn. 2012. "Misperceptions of Climate-Change Risk as Barriers to Climate-Change Adaptation: A Case Study from the Rewa Delta, Fiji." *Climatic Change* 110, no. 1: 169–186.

Lau, Jacqueline, Danika Kleiber, Sarah Lawless and Philippa Cohen. 2021. "Gender Equality in Climate Policy and Practice Hindered by Assumptions." *Nature Climate Change* 11, no. 3: 186–192.

Leustean, Lucian. 2022. "Russia's Invasion of Ukraine: The First Religious War in the 21st Century." *LSE Religion and Global Society Blog.* Accessed on June 21, 2022. https://blogs.lse.ac.uk/religionglobalsociety/2022/03/russias-invasion-of-ukraine-the-first-religious-war-in-the-21st-century/.

Luetz, Johannes and Patrick Nunn. 2020. "Climate Change Adaptation in the Pacific Islands: A Review of Faith-Engaged Approaches and Opportunities." In *Managing Climate Change Adaptation in the Pacific Region*, edited by Walter Leal, 293–311. Cham: Springer.

Lynch, Cecelia. 2011. "Religious Humanitarianism and the Global Politics of Secularism." In *Rethinking Secularism*, edited by Craig Calhoun, Mark Juergensmeyer and Jonathan van Antwerpen, 204–224. Oxford: Oxford University Press.

Lynch, Cecelia and Tanya Schwarz. 2016. "Humanitarianism's Proselytism Problem." *International Studies Quarterly* 60, no. 4: 636–646.

## 134 Bibliography

Ma, Y., Z. Pan, F. Yu, Y. Shi and Y. Y. Siu. 2018. "Constructing Rohingya Identity: An Analysis of Media Process and Self-Representations." *Global Media Journal* 16, no. 31: 1–11.

Maddox, Marion. 2010. "Indigenous Religion in Secular Australia." *Department of the Parliamentary Library, Information and Research Service.* Canberra: Parliament of Australia. Accessed on December 2, 2021. https://www.aph.gov.au/binaries/library/pubs/rp/1999-2000/2000rpl1.pdf.

Mahmood, Saba. 2016. *Religion in a Secular Age: A Minority Report.* Princeton: Princeton University Press.

Mahmood, Saba and Peter Danchin. 2014. "Immunity or Regulation? Antinomies of Religious Freedom." *The South Atlantic Quarterly* 113, no. 1: 129–159.

Mamdani, Mahmood. 2002. "Good Muslim, Bad Muslim: A Political Perspective on Culture and Terrorism." *American Anthropologist* 104, no. 3: 766–775.

Mandaville, Peter. 2021. "Right-Sizing Religion and Religious Engagement in Diplomacy and Development." *The Review of Faith & International Affairs* 19, no. 1: 92–97.

Mandaville, Peter. 2022. "How Putin Turned Religion's 'Sharp Power' Against Ukraine." *United States Institute for Peace.* February 9, 2022. Accessed on June 22, 2022. https://www.usip.org/publications/2022/02/how-putin-turned-religions-sharp-power-against-ukraine.

Mandaville, Peter and Melissa Nozell. "Engaging Religion and Religious Actors in Countering Violent Extremism." *Special Report 413.* August 2017. Washington, DC: United States Institute for Peace.

Marshall, Katherine and Lucy Keough. 2004. *Mind, Heart, and Soul in the Fight against Poverty.* Washington, DC: World Bank.

Matthies-Boon, Vivienne. 2017. "Shattered Worlds: Political Trauma amongst Young Activists in Post-revolutionary Egypt." *The Journal of North African Studies* 22, no. 4: 620–644.

Mavelli, Luca. 2011. "Security and Secularization in International Relations." *European Journal of International Relations* 18, no. 1: 177–199.

Mavelli, Luca. 2012. *Europe's Encounter with Islam: The Secular and the Postsecular.* London: Routledge.

McGregor-Lowndes, Myles and Frances Hannah 2021. "Watkins v Commissioner for Corporate Affairs [2021] Sacat 10." *ACPNS Legal Reports Series.* Accessed on June 7, 2022. https://eprints.qut.edu.au/211915/1/2021_44_Watkins_v_Commissioner_for_Corporate_Affairs_2021_SACAT_10.pdf.

McGuirk, Siobhán and Max Niedzwiecki. 2016. "Loving God vs. Wrathful God: Religion and LGBT Forced Migration." In *The Refugee Crisis and Religion: Secularism, Security and Hospitality in Question*, edited by Luca Mavelli and Erin Kate Wilson, 223–239. London: Rowman and Littlefield International.

McMichael, Philip and Heloise Weber. 2021. *Development and Social Change: A Global Perspective.* London: Sage.

## Bibliography   135

Meaney, Thomas. "Putin Wants a Clash of Civilizations. Is 'The West' Falling for It?" *The New York Times.* March 11, 2022. Accessed on June 22, 2022. https://www.nytimes.com/2022/03/11/opinion/nato-russia-the-west-ukraine.html.

Mearsheimer, John. 2014. "Why the Ukraine Crisis Is the West's Fault." *Foreign Affairs* 93, no. 5: 1–12.

Menchik, Jeremy. 2015. *Islam and Democracy in Indonesia: Tolerance without Liberalism.* Cambridge: Cambridge University Press.

Mepschen, Paul, Jan Willem Duyvendak and Evelien Tonkens. 2010. "Sexual Politics, Orientalism and Multicultural Citizenship in the Netherlands." *Sociology* 44, no. 5: 962–979.

Merry, Sally Engle. 2006. "Transnational Human Rights and Local Activism: Mapping the Middle." *American Anthropologist* 108, no. 1: 38–51.

Mikhailovich, Katja and Alexandra Pavli, assisted by Cathryn McConaghy and Nathaniel Ward. 2011. *Freedom of Religion, Belief, and Indigenous Spirituality, Practice, and Cultural Rights.* Canberra: Centre for Education, Poverty and Social Inclusion, Faculty of Education, University of Canberra. Accessed on June 12, 2022. https://humanrights.gov.au/sites/default/files/content/frb/papers/Indigenous%20Spirituality%20FINAL%20May%202011.pdf.

Mofya, Teddy. 2022. "Channels of Hope COVID-19 Vaccines Model Elates Faith & Traditional Leaders." *World Vision.* Accessed on June 27, 2022. https://www.wvi.org/stories/faith-and-development/channels-hope-covid-19-vaccines-model-elates-faith-traditional.

Mortreux, Colette and Jon Barnett. 2009. "Climate Change, Migration and Adaptation in Funafuti, Tuvalu." *Global Environmental Change* 19, no. 1: 105–112.

Mudde, Cas. 2019. *The Far Right Today.* London: Polity Press.

Murphy, Katherine. 2021. "Scott Morrison Wants Australians to Know He's a Pentecostal Christian, But Questions about It Make Him Uneasy." *The Guardian.* April 20, 2021. Accessed on June 27, 2022. https://www.theguardian.com/australia-news/2021/may/01/scott-morrison-wants-australians-to-know-hes-a-pentecostal-christian-but-questions-about-it-make-him-uneasy.

Myint-U, Thant. 2019. "Not a Single Year's Peace: Thant Myint-U on Burma's Problems." *London Review of Books* 41, no. 22. https://lrb.co.uk/the-paper/v41/n22/thant-myint-u/not-a-single-year-s-peace.

Ndlovu-Gatsheni, Sabelo. 2015. "Decoloniality as the Future of Africa." *History Compass* 13, no. 10: 485–496.

Nelson, Matthew. 2020a. "Pandemic Politics in South Asia: Muslims and Democracy. Transatlantic Policy Network on Religion and Diplomacy Report." Accessed on October 8, 2020. https://religionanddiplomacy.org.uk/wp-content/uploads/2020/09/TPNRD-Nelson-Pandemic-Politics-in-South-Asia.pdf.

## 136 Bibliography

Nelson, Matthew. 2020b. "Constitutional Migration and the Meaning of Religious Freedom: From Ireland and India to the Islamic Republic of Pakistan." *Journal of Asian Studies* 79, no. 1: 129–154.

Ngo, May. 2018. *Between Humanitarianism and Evangelism in Faith-Based Organisations: A Case from the African Migration Route.* London: Routledge.

Norgaard, Kari. 2011. *Living in Denial: Climate Change, Emotions and Everyday Life.* Boston, MA: MIT Press.

Nunn, Patrick. 2017. "Sidelining God: Why Secular Climate Projects in the Pacific Islands are Failing." *The Conversation.* May 16, 2017. Accessed on June 27, 2022. https://theconversation.com/sidelining-god-why-secular-climate-projects-in-the-pacific-islands-are-failing-77623.

Nunn, Patrick, Kate Mulgrew, Bridie Scott-Parker, Donald Hine, Anthony Marks, Doug Mahar and Jack Maebuta. 2016. "Spirituality and Attitudes towards Nature in the Pacific Islands: Insights for Enabling Climate-Change Adaptation." *Climatic Change* 136: 477–493.

O'Beara, Fearghas. 2022. "Russia's War on Ukraine: The Religious Dimension." *European Parliamentary Research Service.* Accessed on June 23, 2022. https://www.europarl.europa.eu/RegData/etudes/ATAG/2022/729355/EPRS_ATA(2022)729355_EN.pdf.

Office of International Religious Freedom. "2021 Report on International Religious Freedom." *U.S. Department of State.* June 2, 2022. https://www.state.gov/reports/2021-report-on-international-religious-freedom/.

O'Grady, Siobhan. "Sorry, Dutch Pastafarians, But You Still Can't Wear a Colander on Your Government ID...Yet." *The Washington Post.* August 17, 2018. Accessed on May 23, 2022. https://go.gale.com/ps/i.do?p=AONE&sw=w&issn=&v=2.1&it=r&id=GALE%7CA550592886&sid=-googleScholar&linkaccess=fulltext&userGroupName=anon%7Ecba3ffcb.

O'Neill, Saffron and Sophie Nicholson-Cole. 2009. "'Fear Won't Do it': Promoting Positive Engagement with Climate Change through Visual and Iconic Representations." *Science Communication* 30, no. 3: 355–379.

Pacific Conference of Churches. 2022. "Our Member Churches." Accessed on June 27, 2022. https://www.pacificconferenceofchurches.org/about-us/our-member-churches/.

Pearson, Alexander. 2018. "German Court Allows Courtroom Headscarf Ban." *Deutsche Welle (DW).* March 7, 2018. Accessed on June 12, 2022. https://www.dw.com/en/german-court-allows-courtroom-headscarf-ban/a-42857656.

Petersen, Marie Juul. 2021. "The International Promotion of Freedom of Religion or Belief: Key Debates and Divides." In *Handbook on Religion and International Relations,* edited by Jeffrey Haynes, 215–230. Cheltenham: Edward Elgar Publishing.

Petheram, Lisa, Kerstin Zander, Bruce Campbell, Chris High and Natasha Stacey. 2010. "'Strange Changes': Indigenous Perspectives of Climate Change and Adaptation in NE Arnhem Land (Australia)." *Global Environmental Change* 20, no. 4: 681–692.

Philpott, Daniel. 2009. "Has the Study of Global Politics Found Religion?" *Annual Review of Political Science* 12: 183–202.

## Bibliography 137

Philpott, Daniel. 2013. "Religious Freedom and Peacebuilding: May I Introduce You Two?" *The Review of Faith & International Affairs* 11, no. 1: 31–37.

Philpott, Daniel and Timothy Samuel Shah. 2016. "In Defense of Religious Freedom: New Critics of a Beleaguered Human Right." *Journal of Law and Religion* 31, no. 3: 380–395.

Piggott-McKellar, Annah, Karen McNamara, Patrick Nunn and James Watson. 2019. "What Are the Barriers to Successful Community-Based Climate Change Adaptation? A Review of Grey Literature." *Local Environment* 24, no. 4: 374–390.

Povinelli, Elizabeth. 1995. "Do Rocks Listen? The Cultural Politics of Apprehending Australian Aboriginal Labor." *American Anthropologist* 97, no. 3: 505–518.

Prasse-Freeman, Elliott and Ko Kabya. 2021. "Revolutionary Responses to the Myanmar Coup." *Anthropology Today* 37, no. 3: 1–2.

Quinn, Ben. 2016. "French Police Make Woman Remove Clothing on Nice Beach Following Burkini Ban." *The Guardian.* August 24, 2016. Accessed on June 12, 2022. https://www.theguardian.com/world/2016/aug/24/french-police-make-woman-remove-burkini-on-nice-beach.

Raad van State. 2018. "'Pastafarianism' Is Not a Religion." August 15, 2018. Accessed on June 7, 2022. https://www.raadvanstate.nl/@112548/past afarianism-not/.

Ramos, Jennifer and Priscilla Torres. 2020. "The Right Transmission: Understanding Global Diffusion of the Far-Right." *Populism* 3, no. 1: 87–120.

Rose, Deborah Bird. 1998. "Consciousness and Responsibility in an Australian Aboriginal Religion." In *Traditional Aboriginal Society*, edited by William Howell Edwards, 2nd Edition. Melbourne: Macmillan Education.

Rots, Aike. 2015. "Sacred Forests, Sacred Nation: The Shinto Environmentalist Paradigm and the Rediscovery of 'Chinju no Mori'." *Japanese Journal of Religious Studies* 42, no. 2: 205–233.

Roy, Olivier. 2022. "Ukraine and the Clash of Civilisations Theory: An Interview with Olivier Roy." *European University Institute.* March 10, 2022. Accessed on June 23, 2022. https://www.eui.eu/news-hub?id=ukraine-and-the-clash-of-civilisation-theory-an-interview-with-oliver-roy.

Saeed, Sadia. 2016. *Politics of Desecularization: Law and the Minority Question in Pakistan.* New York: Cambridge University Press.

Said, Edward. 1978. *Orientalism: Western Conceptions of the Orient.* London and New York: Routledge Kegan Paul.

Sajjad, Tazreena. 2022. "Ukrainian Refugees Are Welcomed with Open Arms – Not So with People Fleeing Other War-Torn Countries." *The Conversation.* March 9, 2022. Accessed on June 22, 2022. https://theconversation.com/ukrainian-refugees-are-welcomed-with-open-arms-not-so-with-people-fleeing-other-war-torn-countries-178491.

Schmid, Alex. 2013. "Radicalisation, De-radicalisation, Counter-Radicalisation: A Conceptual Discussion and Literature Review." *ICCT Research Paper* 4, no. 2. The Hague: The International Centre for Counter-Terrorism.

138   *Bibliography*

Schonthal, Benjamin. 2015. "Ceylon/Sri Lanka: The Politics of Religious Freedom and the End of Empire." In *Politics of Religious Freedom*, edited by Winnifred Fallers Sullivan, Elizabeth Shakman Hurd, Saba Mahmood and Peter Danchin, 149–157. Chicago: Chicago University Press.

Scott, Joan Wallach. 2007. *The Politics of the Veil*. Princeton: Princeton University Press.

Scott, Joan Wallach. 2018. *Sex and Secularism*. Princeton: Princeton University Press.

Selim, George. 2016. "Approaches for Countering Violent Extremism at Home and Abroad." *Annals of the American Academy of Political and Social Science* 668, no. 1: 94–101.

Sharp, Nonie. 1998. "Mabo's Law in Court: The Religious Background to the Mabo Case." In *Religious Business: Australian Aboriginal Spirituality*, edited by Max Charlesworth, 176–202. New York: Cambridge University Press.

Simon, Reeva Specter and Eleanor Tejirian. 2004. "Introduction – The Creation of Iraq: The Frontier State." In *The Creation of Iraq 1914–1921*, edited by Reeva Specter Simon and Eleanor Tejirian, 1–18. New York: Columbia University Press.

de Sousa Santos, Boaventura. 2014. *Epistemologies of the South: Justice against Epistemicide*. London: Routledge.

Staudenmaier, Rebecca. 2018. "Germany: Bavaria's Controversial Cross Rule Goes into Effect." *Deutsche Welle (DW)*. May 31, 2018. Accessed on June 12, 2022. https://www.dw.com/en/germany-bavarias-controversial-cross-rule-goes-into-effect/a-44027316.

Stevenson, Jonathan. 2019. "Right-Wing Extremism and the Terrorist Threat." *Survival* 61, no.1: 233–244.

Suleman, Arsalan. 2018. "Return of the Clash: Operationalizing a Tainted Worldview." *The Washington Quarterly* 40, no. 4: 49–70.

Sullivan, Winnifred Fallers. 2005. *The Impossibility of Religious Freedom*. Princeton: Princeton University Press.

Swearer, Donald. 2006. "An Assessment of Buddhist Eco-Philosophy." *Harvard Theological Review* 99, no. 2: 123–137.

Tanner, Thomas and Leo Horn-Phathanothai. 2014. *Climate Change and Development*. London: Routledge.

Tarusarira, Joram. 2022. "Religious Environmental Sensemaking in Climate-Induced Conflicts." *Religions* 13, no. 3: 204. https://doi.org/10.3390/rel13030204.

Thames, Knox. 2022. "Defending Religion in Ukraine – Russia's Putin Distorts Shared Christian Roots to Justify War." *Fox News*. March 6, 2022. Accessed on June 22, 2022. https://www.foxnews.com/opinion/defending-religion-ukraine-russia-putin-knox-thames.

Tomalin, Emma. 2021. "Religions and Development: A Paradigm Shift or Business as Usual?" *Religion* 51, no. 1: 105–124.

## Bibliography 139

UNFPA. 2009. *Guidelines for Engaging Faith-Based Organisation (FBOs) as Agents of Change.* UNFPA. https://www.unfpa.org/resources/guidelines-engaging-faith-based-organisations-fbo-agents-change.

UNHCR. 2014. *On Faith-Based Organizations, Local Faith Communities and Faith Leaders.* Geneva: United Nations High Commissioner for Refugees. https://www.unhcr.org/protection/hcdialogue%20/539ef28b9/partnership-note-faith-based-organizations-local-faith-communities-faith.html.

UNHCR. 2022. *Global Trends: Forced Displacement in 2021.* Copenhagen: United Nations High Commissioner for Refugees. Accessed on June 21, 2022. https://www.unhcr.org/publications/brochures/62a9d1494/global-trends-report-2021.html.

United States Government Department of State. 2022. "Vietnam." *International Religious Freedom Report 2021.* Accessed on June 20, 2022. https://www.state.gov/reports/2021-report-on-international-religious-freedom/vietnam/.

Veldman, Robin. 2019. *The Gospel of Climate Skepticism. Why Evangelical Christians Oppose Action on Climate Change.* Oakland, CA: University of California Press.

Viveiros de Castro, Eduardo. 2013. "The Relative Native." Translated by Julia Sauma and Martin Holbraad. *Hau: Journal of Ethnographic Theory* 3, no. 3: 473–502.

Wahlquist, Calla. 2020. "Rio Tinto Blasts 46,000-Year-Old Aboriginal Site to Expand Iron Ore Mine." *The Guardian.* May 26, 2020. Accessed on June 12, 2022. https://www.theguardian.com/australia-news/2020/may/26/rio-tinto-blasts-46000-year-old-aboriginal-site-to-expand-iron-ore-mine.

Wainscott, Ann. 2019. *Engaging the Post-ISIS Iraqi Religious Landscape for Peace and Reconciliation.* Washington, DC: United States Institute of Peace.

Walthausen, Abby. 2019. "On Victor Hugo's Posthumous Career as a Religious Prophet: How the Author of *Les Misérables* Became a Fixture of Cao Dai." *Literary Hub.* August 21, 2019. Accessed on June 20, 2022. https://lithub.com/on-victor-hugos-posthumous-career-as-a-religious-prophet/.

Weiner, James. 2002. "Religion, Belief and Action: The Case of Ngarrindjeri 'Women's Business' on Hindmarsh Island, South Australia 1994–1996." *The Australian Journal of Anthropology* 13, no. 1: 51–71.

Wenger, Tisa. 2011. "Indian Dances and the Politics of Religious Freedom, 1870–1930." *Journal of the American Academy of Religion* 79, no. 4: 850–878.

White, Lynn. 1967. "The Historical Roots of Our Ecological Crisis." *Science* 155, no. 3767: 1203–1207.

Wieringa, Saskia. 2015. "Gender Harmony and the Happy Family." *South East Asia Research* 23, no. 1: 27–44.

Wilkinson, Olivia. 2020. *Secular and Religious Dynamics in Humanitarian Response.* London: Routledge.

Williams, Andrew, Paul Cloke and Samuel Thomas. 2012. "Co-Constituting Neoliberalism: Faith-Based Organisations, Co-Option, and Resistance in the UK." *Environment and Planning A: Economy and Space* 44, no. 6: 1479–1501.

## Bibliography

Wilson, Erin Kate. 2012. *After Secularism: Rethinking Religion in Global Politics*. Basingstoke: Palgrave.

Wilson, Erin Kate. 2017. "'Power Differences and the Power of Difference': The Dominance of Secularism as Ontological Injustice." *Globalizations* 14, no. 7: 1076–1093.

Wilson, Erin Kate. 2022a. "Cast Out Fear: Secularism (In)Security and the Politics of Climate Change." In *Climate Politics and the Power of Religion*, edited by Evan Berry, 97–121. Bloomington, IN: Indiana University Press.

Wilson, Erin Kate. 2022b. "Blurring Boundaries or Deepening Discourses on FoRB? From Global to Local and Back Again." *Review of Faith and International Affairs* 20, no. 2: 69–80.

Wilson, Erin Kate and Luca Mavelli. 2016. "Taking Responsibility: Sociodicy, Solidarity, and Religious-Sensitive Policymaking in the Global Politics of Migration." In *Intersections of Religion and Migration*, edited by Jennifer Saunders, Elena Fiddian-Qasmiyeh and Susanna Snyder, 261–284. New York: Palgrave Macmillan.Wilson, Lydia. 2017. "Understanding the Appeal of ISIS." *New England Journal of Public Policy* 29, no. 1: Article 5. https://scholarworks.umb.edu/nejpp/vol29/iss1/5.

Wilson, Lydia. 2021. "Gone to Waste: the 'CVE' Industry after 9/11." *New Lines Magazine.* Accessed on April 15, 2022. https://newlinesmag.com/argument/understanding-the-lure-of-islamism-is-more-complex-than-the-experts-would-have-you-believe/.

Wohlrab-Sahr, Monika and Marion Burchardt. 2012. "Multiple Secularities: Toward a Cultural Sociology of Secular Modernities." *Comparative Sociology* 11, no. 6: 875–909.

World Council of Churches. 2009. "Pacific Church Leaders' Statement." Accessed on June 27, 2022. https://www.oikoumene.org/resources/documents/pacific-church-leaders-statement.

World Health Organisation. 2021. "Violence against Women Prevalence Estimates, 2018 – Global Fact Sheet." Accessed on June 22, 2022. https://www.who.int/publications/i/item/WHO-SRH-21.6.

World Vision International. 2016. "Channels of Hope: An Effective Behaviour Change and Advocacy Methodology for Faith Leaders and Faith Communities." *World Vision International.* Accessed on June 27, 2022. https://www.wvi.org/sites/default/files/Channels_of_Hope_project_model.pdf.

Yeboah, Stephen. "Kofi Annan Supports the Encyclical on Climate Change." *LinkedIn.* June 18, 2015. https://www.linkedin.com/pulse/kofi-annan-supports-encyclical-climate-change-stephen-yeboah/.

Yunupingu, Galarrwuy. 1996. "Concepts of Land and Spirituality." In *Aboriginal Spirituality: Past, Present, Future*, edited by A. Pattel-Gray, 4–10. Blackburn: Harper Collins.

Zaman, Tahir. 2016. *Islamic Traditions of Refuge in the Crises of Iraq and Syria*. London: Springer.

# Index

Note: **Bold** page numbers refer to tables; *Italic* page numbers refer to figures and page numbers followed by "n" denote endnotes.

ACTED *see* Agency for Technical Cooperation and Development (ACTED)
actors 26–28, *39,* 42, 49–51, 58–59, 63, 99
added value 62, 63, 66
Afghanistan wars 29, 34
Agency for Technical Cooperation and Development (ACTED) 89
Ahmadiyya community 76, 107–108
AJP *see* Alliance for Justice and Peace (AJP)
Alevis in Turkey 108
Alexandrina council 113
Alliance for Justice and Peace (AJP) 105–106
Al-Marashi, Ibrahim 52
"American-style" religious freedom 101
Anders Breivik killings in Norway 55
Anglo-Burmese wars 40
Annan, Kofi 65
antagonism 68
anti-Catholic 59
anti-colonial struggles 6, 41, 44
anti-immigrant 55, 60
anti-immigration 56–58
anti-Indian sentiment 41, 42
anti-Islam/anti-Muslim 42, 55, 57, *58,* 60
Arab Sunni population 52
Arakan Rohingya Salvation Army (ARSA) 45

ARSA *see* Arakan Rohingya Salvation Army (ARSA)
Article 260, akistani constitution 108
Article 9, European Convention on Human Rights 116
Article 18, Universal Declaration of Human Rights 103
"Asian Values" debate 98
assertive secularisms 10
2019 attack, Christchurch Mosque 36, 55
2021 attack, US capitol building 36, 55
Aung San Suu Kyi 39–41, 43
Australia 96, 110, 111, 114
Australian spirituality 114
Austrian Freedom Party 59
authenticity 113

Ba'ath party 49, 52
Bavaria government 119
1995 Beijing Platform for Action 69
Bertana, Amanda 84, 85
Bible 30
Biden administration: Iraq, US troops 46
black magic 105
British 34; Afghanistan wars 34; Iraq wars 34; policy and military establishment 18–19; secular security imaginary 18; secular ways of war 34

142    *Index*

British Expeditionary Forces 41
British India 41
broader development 62
broader human rights agenda 78
broader secular paradigms 63
broad terminology 55
Buddha's dispensation (teachings) 43
Buddhism 41, 44, 81, 83
Buddhist nationalism 40–43, 77;
    monk-initiated movements 43;
    protecting Myanmar 44
Burman Buddhist majority 42, 43
Burmese Army 41
Bush, George W. 46

Cao Dai 6, *7*, 8
Caodaism 6, 8
Catholic Church 81
certain ambivalences 18
CFSM *see* Church of the Flying
    Spaghetti Monster (CFSM)
Channels of Hope Gender (CoHG)
    programme 73–76
Christian evangelism 103
Christianity 1, 10, 12, 20, 80, 83
Christians 30, 45, 50, 74, 77, 102
Christian West 59
Church of the Flying Spaghetti
    Monster (CFSM) 92, *93*, 95
Cirebon 77, 78, 104
civilisational identity 12
civilisations: conceptualisation of 12;
    Orthodox civilisation 12
civil religion 30
civil society practitioners 2
Clarke, Gerard 71
Clash of Civilisations (CoC) 12–13
clearance operations 45
climate adaptation 85, 86
climate change 64, 80–82, 85, 111
climate denialism 57
Coalition partners 50, 53
Coalition Provisional authority 52
CoC *see* Clash of Civilisations (CoC)
Cold War 12; power struggles 47
colonial Burma 40–41
colonial interventions 47
Commonwealth Aboriginal and
    Torres Strait Islander Heritage
    Protection Act 110

community 3, 69, 74, 84, 95, 104, 110
community-based settings 63
community organisations 77
conflict 12, 15, 37, 80; religion's
    role in 13; "top-down" approach
    13; transformation 68; in
    Ukraine 13
Confucian 77
Congregational or Community Hope
    Action Teams (CHATs) 74
Constitution of the Irish
    Republic 107
context 22, 23, *24, 35,* 38, 96;
    conceptualisations of 25;
    humanitarianism 69; international
    development 69; intersectional
    understanding *25*
contextually analysis 22
Coptic Christians in Egypt 108
corrupt elite 56
cosmopolitan spirituality 7, 8
countering violent extremism (CVE)
    23, 33, 35, 47, 68, 108
COVID-19 vaccination 57, 74
Cox, Jo 36, 55
criminalisation 29
criticism 71
cross-cultural encounter 4
cultural heritage 10
cultural taboos 69
CVE *see* countering violent
    extremism (CVE)
cyber-security 12

*Dahlab v Switzerland* case 29, 116,
    117, **118**
"de-Baathification" policy 52
deep culture 30
developed countries 64
"developing" areas 64
development 28, 63; concept and
    practice 86; idea of 64
disrupt public order 107
diversity 77, 83, 104
domestic policies 36
domestic welfare provision 67
dominant secular paradigms 63
donor priorities 85
"Dreaming" 111
dubious theory 12

## Index   143

East India Company 40
Ebola 74
ECJ *see* European Court of Justice (ECJ)
economic consequences 12
economic inequality 65
ECtHR *see* European Court of Human Rights (ECtHR)
Edkins, Jenny 19
emergency humanitarian relief 65
"empirical verifiability" 113
environments 37
Epiphany 4–5
epistemological violence 21
ethnicity 8
ethnic minority groups 41
ethno-religious groups 45, 46
Euro-American contexts 34, 47, 50, 61n1
Euro-American spiritualists 7
European Court of Human Rights (ECtHR) 29, 115–118
European Court of Justice (ECJ) 115
European public spheres 115–119
European Union (EU) 14; ideological threads 57; religious diplomacy 14
exclusion 21
external observers 32
extreme right religious 56, 58
extremism 33, 36, 37, 45; anti-social behaviours 38; far-right extremism 36, 37; Islamist extremism 36, 38, 47, 58, 60; militant Islamist extremism 42; nationalist extremism 36; right-wing extremism 15; Shia extremism 54; Sunni extremism 54; violent extremism 36, 46
extremist far-right violence 60

Fahmina 76–80, 104
faith 71
faith-based organisations 62, 65, 71, 90
far-right extremism 36, 37, 56; definition of 56–58; narratives 59–60; phenomenon of 57; political ideological spectrum 56; religious actors 58–59; religious identity 59; transnational rise of 55–56

far-right sovereign citizen movements 57
FoRB *see* freedom of religion or belief (FoRB)
forced migration 86–90
foreign policy 23, 103
Foxeus, Niklas 42
Francis (Pope) 14, 81
freedom of religion or belief (FoRB) 19, 47, 95, 96, 101–104; foreign policy 107; indigenous rights 108–115; in Indonesia and India 104–106; international diplomacy 107; minority rights 106–109
Freeman, Michael 96
French imperial rule 6
French Republicanism 8
"The Future of Religion" 3

gay Muslim refugees 29
gender-based violence 64, 69, 73, 75, 86
gender equality 28, 64, 69, 72–73, 83
gender identities 73, 76
gender inequality 64, 86, 119
gender roles 73–75, 77
genocide 44, 45
geopolitical factors 13
Ghulam Ahmad 107
Global Financial Crisis in 2008 59
global policy developments 23
global political developments 23
global political power 37
global politics: primary actor in 23; religion's place in 20
global power 21, 63
Global Trends report 3
Global War on Terror 46
Gogali, Lian 78, 79
Groningen-based research team 104
Guterres, Antonio 65
Gutkowski, Stacey 18, 34, 35

Harvard Kennedy School 11
hate speech 14
Helfont, Samuel 50
Heritage Protection Act 112
Hindmarsh-Goolwa Bridge 113
Hindmarsh Island case 109–111
Hindu/Hindus 45, 77; majority 106; nationalism 60

144 *Index*

Hinduism 10, 83
hoax religion 92
hope programme 73–76
Hugo, Victor 6; French imperial
 rule 7; *Les Contemplations* 6; *Les
 Miserables* 6; mysticism of 8;
 Napoleon III 7; *Notre Dame de
 Paris* 6
human activity 8, 22
humanitarianism 15, 16, 23, 28, 63,
 64, 69
humanity 80, 81
human rights 28, 78, 80, 96, 97–98,
 101, 106, 120
Huntington, Samuel 12
Hurd, Elizabeth Shakman 35, 47, 107
Hussein, Saddam 46, 50; Ba'ath party
 49; Sunni *vs.* Shia communities 52

identitarian movements 57
identities 28–30, *39,* 44, 52, 59,
 99–100
ideological threads 57
IGOs *see* inter-governmental
 organisations (IGOs)
Imams 45
imperial conflict 47
"incel" (involuntarily celibate)
 extremism 36
"independence and neutrality" 118
India 60
Indian migration 42
Indigenous Australian
 spiritualities 111
indigenous rights 96, 108–115
Indigenous spirituality 112
individual rights 97
Indonesia 76–80; community
 organisations 77; gender equality
 in 79; Muslim-majority democracy
 76; tribal traditions 77
innovative work 19
inquiry 113
insecurity 12, 33, 35, 36, 37, 46, 120
instability 2, 46
institutionalised religion 28
integrated analysis 22
inter-governmental organisations
 (IGOs) 55, 97
internal religious dynamics 3

international aid 65
international community 65
international development 63, 64, 69;
 faith-based actors 71; identities and
 narratives 71; "religion" matters in
 71; religious actors 71
international human rights 19, 20, 97
International Partnership on Religion
 and Development (PaRD) 65
international politics 1, 2, 9, 95
international relations (IR) 2, 4–5,
 8–14; "all or nothing" approach 11;
 analytical framework 21–25; "core
 business" of 31; critical approaches
 **14**; epistemological violence 21;
 secular discipline 8
international security 23, 32
international system 23
inter-religious conflict 47, 107
inter-religious divisions 49
intersectional analysis 22
Iraq 36; Coalition Provisional
 authority 52; "de-Baathification"
 policy 52; ethno-religious groups
 46, 47; Euro-American policies
 47; geopolitics and religion 47;
 imperial conflict 47; insecurity and
 conflict in 46; power and privilege
 in 52; religious authorities 50;
 religious dynamics 49; religious
 leadership in 51; religious space
 in 50; role of religious 50; security
 forces 52; social and political life
 46; socio-political life in 50; socio-
 political situation 46
Iraqi religious landscape 54
Iraqi society 49
Iraq wars 18, 34, 46
irrational belief 66
irrationality 113
"irrational" nature 81
"irregular" conflicts 33
ISIS community 46, 49, 52, 54
Islam 10, 18, 20, 29, 32, 49, 83, 87;
 description of 12; dynamic 18; global
 policy 37; multiple types of 12;
 violent, threat of 38; *see also* Muslim
Islamist extremism 36, 38, 47, 58, 60
Islamophobia 58
Italian court system 117

Jews 58
jihadism 60
Justice Jane Mathews 113

Kalenychenko, Tetiana 14
Kansas School Board 92
Kartinyeri, Doreen Dr. 110, 114
Kelly, Robert 12
Khiêm, Nguyễn Binh 7
Ki-moon, Ban 65
Kissinger, Henry 11
Kozelsky, Mara 13
Kubalkova, Vendulka 8
Kumarangk (Hindmarsh Island)
  controversy 112, 114; *see also*
  Hindmarsh Island case
Kuru, Ahmed 9

labour 32
language 69, 71, 78, 101
*Lautsi and others v Italy* case 29, 115,
  116, **118**
leadership 28, 76
"legitimate" religious actor 68
*Les Contemplations* (Hugo) 6
*Les Miserables* (Hugo) 6
LGBTQI+ people 28, 72, 73, 81, 100;
  rights and equality 76
liberal democratic values 10
lived religion 2, 19
local faith communities 71
long-term policy planning 3
Luetz, Johannes 82

MaBaTha *see* Organization for the
  Protection of Race/Nation and
  Religion (MaBaTha)
Maddox, Marion 112, 113
Mahmood, Saba 47, 107, 108
mainstream IR analysis 20, 23
marginalisation 21, 52
*margin of appreciation* rule 118
Mathews' Inquiry 113
Mavelli, Luca 34, 35
McEvoy, Kathleen 94, 95
meaning-making frameworks 20, 30,
  111, 114
Mearsheimer, John 11
Mensen met een Missie (MM) 77
mental health 87, 88, 111

Mental Health and Psychosocial
  Support (MHPSS) 88, 90
MHPSS *see* Mental Health and
  Psychosocial Support (MHPSS)
middle-income countries 64
migration 28, 29, 64, 68, 81
militant Islamist extremism 42
2021 Military Coup in Myanmar
  39–40
military strategy 33
Min Aung Hlaing 39, 41, 44
minority religions 8, 116
minority rights 96, 106–109
misogyny 73
Moana Declaration in 2009 83, 91n4
modern Iraqi state 48
modern secular state 34
Morrison, Scott 27–28
Mosintuwu 76–80, 77, 78, 79
969 movement 43
Mudde, Cas 56, 59
multi-faith communities 74
Muslim 28, 29, 45, 58, 68, 74, 102,
  108; anti-Western narratives 78;
  community 106; gender equality
  78; legal trainee 118; majority
  countries 36; minorities 36;
  populations 13; violence 108;
  women's rights 10, 78, 119; *see also*
  Islam
Muslim ban 29
mutual instrumentalisation 14
Myanmar 25, 36; anti-colonial
  struggle 41; anti-Indian response
  41; anti-Muslim sentiment
  42; Buddhist nationalism in
  40–41; clearance operations 45;
  democratic governance 40; ethnic
  minority groups 41; genocide
  45; Indian migration 42; map of
  *42*; national identity 44; place of
  religion in 40; political agenda
  44; political unrest and instability
  40; pro-democracy movement 44;
  Rohingya minority 41; socio-
  political landscape 45

Narikoso man 85
narratives 30, *39,* 45, 52–53, 59–60,
  100–101

146 *Index*

"national emergency" 39
national interest 8
nationalist extremism 36
National League for Democracy
    (NLD) party 39, 44
national media campaign 78
National Socialist Underground
    terror cell 59
NATO expansion 11
natural disasters 65
nature 80, 81
Nelson, Matthew 107
neo-colonial agendas 101
neo-fascism 56, 57
neoliberalism 67
neo-Nazi movements 57
Netherlands 28
neutrality 66
*Ngaji Rasa* (I am you, you are me) 104
Ngarrindjeri community 112
Ngarrindjeri tradition 110
Ngarrindjeri women 110, 111, 112, 113
NGOs *see* non-governmental
    organisations (NGOs)
NIC *see* US National Intelligence
    Council (NIC)
NLD party *see* National League for
    Democracy (NLD) party
non-belief 54
"non-Burmese" people 41, 44
non-governmental organisations
    (NGOs) 3, 66, 67, 71, 73, 97
non-verbal communication 30
*Notre Dame de Paris* (Hugo) 6
Nunn, Patrick 82

organisation 75, 105; community
    organisations 77; faith-based
    organisations 62, 65, 71, 90;
    terrorist organisations 71
Organization for the Protection
    of Race/Nation and Religion
    (MaBaTha) 43, 44
Orientalist 38
Orthodox Christianity 12–13
Orthodox Church 14
"Orthodox" civilisation 12
Orthodox World 14
"Other" 34
Ottoman rule 48

Pacific, climate adaptation 82–83
Pacific Conference of Churches
    (PCC) 83, 84
Pakistan 96; Ahmadiyya community
    107–108; politics and public life
    108; via India 107
Palestinian Refugee Camp 88, *89*
passive secularisms 9–10
Pastafarianism 92
patriarchy 73
PCC *see* Pacific Conference of
    Churches (PCC)
peacebuilding 68, 80
peasant political movement 6
Pentecostals 27
people seeking asylum: religio-racial
    identities of 29
perform discursive violence 57
perhaps obvious 1
physical health 111
physical violence 57
Piggott-McKellar, Annah 83
pluralism 104
policymakers 2, 5
policy terminology 56
political ideology 5, 9
political revolutionary movements 8
political secularisms 9, 35
politico-religious movement 8
populism 56
Poso 78
post-Cold War era 12
post-conflict Iraq 46
post-9/11 environment 13, 55; anti-
    immigrant stance 55; anti-Muslim
    attitudes 55
post-ISIS environment 54
post-war Iraqi politics 53
post-World War II 66
poverty reduction 65, 68, 80
power 8; politics 12; relationships 25,
    29; vacuum 46
practitioners 5
pre-existing narratives 37
pre-existing understanding 1
primary actor 23
pro-Buddhism 44
pro-Buddhist laws 43
pro-democracy movement 44
Prophet Muhammad 107, 108

Protestant Christian NGO 30, 74
public imagination 13
public life 9, 10
public sphere 8, 10
Putin, Vladimir 12; civilisational identity 12; framing and justification 13; Russia-Ukraine conflict 11–12

racism 56
radical right 56
"rational" science 66
recruitment method 53
refugee crisis 28, 59, 68, 86
"regular" wars 33
reinterpreting religious texts 75
relearning religion 21–25
religion 1; actors 26–28; "added value" of 62, 63; category of 6, 20; and climate change 80; critical analysis 19, 21; critical approaches **14**; definition of 20; entanglements 20; examination of 20; fixed idea of 2; and global politics 4; identities 28–30; in international politics 9; and international relations 8–14; intersectional analysis of 22; narratives 30; for public life 9; role in conflict 32; secular assumptions 49; secularist approaches *11*; strategic assessment 3; *see also individual entities*
Religions for Peace Myanmar 44
religio-political community 41, 53
religio-racial identity 55, 58
religious affiliation 72
religious authority 50
religious beliefs 13
religious believers 5
religious diplomacy 14
religious dynamics 13
religious freedom 102–104, 120
religious identity 26, 106; socio-political importance 47
religious institutions 3, 27
religious issues 3
religious liberty 102
religious symbols 10
religious violence 35
Republican and Democratic parties 30

republicanism 6
responsibility 81
revolutionary insight 19
right-sizing religion 20
right-wing 36
right-wing extremism 15
right-wing populism 56
*Roe v Wade* 119
Rohingya minority 41, 42, 44, 45
Rohingya Muslim minority 43
Royal Commission 112, 113
Roy, Olivier 12
Russian religion 12
Russia-Ukraine conflict 11–12

SACAT *see* South Australia Civil and Administrative Tribunal (SACAT)
*sangha* (monastic community) 43
scepticism 29, 84, 103
Scott, Joan 119
SDGs *see* Sustainable Development Goals (SDGs)
"secret women's business" 112
secular: development projects 66; discipline 8; factors 36; feminist attitudes 73; ideologies 10; ways of war 33–39
secular bias 62–63
secularisms 9, 18, 34, 35, 66, 73, 91n3, 115; assertive secularisms 10; passive secularisms 9–10; political secularisms 9; secular ideologies 10
secular states 95, 96
secular tendency 113
"secular ways of war" 34
security 8, 12, 15, 23, 33, 34, 35
security agenda 55
security policy 13
self-identification 26
self-identify 58
settler colonial governments 109
sexism 73
sexuality 73
Shia 76; community 53; extremism 54; majority 48
Shia Muslims 49
Shia Pilgrimage *51*
Shintoism 81
SIDS *see* Small Island Developing States (SIDS)

148 *Index*

*Silaturahmi* (gathering) 104
single-issue extremists 57
al-Sistani, Grand Ayatollah 50
Small Island Developing States
(SIDS) 81–83
social media 53
socio-political arrangements 23
socio-political issues 3
socio-political landscape 45
South Australia Civil and
Administrative Tribunal
(SACAT) 92
South Australian government 113
South Australia's Associations
Incorporation Act 93–94
spiritual heritage 13
spirituality 82, 88, 114
spoken language 30
state authorities 50
State of the Union Addresses 30
state religion 44
states-system 19, 34, 95, 122
stealing jobs 55
structural violence 57
Sulawesi 77, 78
Sunni 76; extremism 54; minority 49, 52
Sunni Muslim 48
Sun Yat-sen 7
superstition 66
Sustainable Development Goals
(SDGs) 64, 65
Sykes-Picot agreement 54
Syria 28
Syrian civil war 86

Taliban 29
Taoist occultism 7
Tatmadaw (Myanmar's military) 39,
44, 45
Ten Commandments 116
terminology 9, 56, 63
terrorism 33, 36, 45, 57
terrorist 29, 68
9/11 terrorist attacks 59
terrorist organisations 71
Theravada Buddhism 7
Tickner, Alan 112
"top-down" approach 13
2018 Toronto van attack 36
traditional media 53
tribal traditions 77

Trump administration: Iraq, US
troops 46; Muslim ban 29
trustworthy 49
"Two Faces of Faith" approach 68

Ukraine 2
*ulama* (scholars) 77
ultranationalist movements 57, 58
under-developed countries 64
Union Solidarity and Development
Party (USDP) 43
Universal Declaration of Human
Rights 98
unlearning religion 5–6
unpacking "religion" 25–26, *27*
UNRWA camps 65
UN Special Rapporteur for FoRB 115
USDP *see* Union Solidarity and
Development Party (USDP)
US-led conflict 46
US National Intelligence Council
(NIC) 3
*uthna-baithna* concept 105

vaguely important 18
Valls, Manuel 119
Velvet Revolution 97
violent extremism 36, 46
violent insurrection 33
vulnerable minority 44

"wars of religion" 34
Watkins, Tanya 93
Western powers 77
White, Lynn 80, 81
white nationalist 36
white working-class communities 59
women: conservative attitudes 77;
equal rights of 75; gender equality
72–73; gender roles 77; religious
leadership in Iraq 51; rights of 28
world politics 22, 38
World Vision (WV) 73–76
World Vision International (WVI) 74
World War I 48, 54
World War II 56
written language 30
WVI *see* World Vision International
(WVI)

Yunupingu, Galarrwuy 111